SAGE was founded in 1965 by Sara Miller McCune to support the dissemination of usable knowledge by publishing innovative and high-quality research and teaching content. Today, we publish over 900 journals, including those of more than 400 learned societies, more than 800 new books per year, and a growing range of library products including archives, data, case studies, reports, and video. SAGE remains majority-owned by our founder, and after Sara's lifetime will become owned by a charitable trust that secures our continued independence.

Los Angeles | London | New Delhi | Singapore | Washington DC | Melbourne

Interruptions
in
Identity

Thank you for choosing a SAGE product!
If you have any comment, observation or feedback,
I would like to personally hear from you.

Please write to me at **contactceo@sagepub.in**

Vivek Mehra, Managing Director and CEO, SAGE India.

Bulk Sales

SAGE India offers special discounts
for purchase of books in bulk.
We also make available special imprints
and excerpts from our books on demand.

For orders and enquiries, write to us at

Marketing Department
SAGE Publications India Pvt Ltd
B1/I-1, Mohan Cooperative Industrial Area
Mathura Road, Post Bag 7
New Delhi 110044, India

E-mail us at **marketing@sagepub.in**

Subscribe to our mailing list
Write to **marketing@sagepub.in**

This book is also available as an e-book.

Interruptions
in
Identity

Engaging with Suicidality
among the Indian Youth

Ambika Singh

Los Angeles | London | New Delhi
Singapore | Washington DC | Melbourne

First published in 2021 by

SAGE Publications India Pvt Ltd
B1/I-1 Mohan Cooperative Industrial Area
Mathura Road, New Delhi 110 044, India
www.sagepub.in

YODA Press
79. Gulmohar Enclave,
New Delhi 110049
www.yodapress.co.in

SAGE Publications Inc
2455 Teller Road
Thousand Oaks, California 91320, USA

SAGE Publications Ltd
1 Oliver's Yard, 55 City Road
London EC1Y 1SP, United Kingdom

SAGE Publications Asia-Pacific Pte Ltd
18 Cross Street #10-10/11/12
China Square Central
Singapore 048423

Published by Vivek Mehra for SAGE Publications India Pvt Ltd. Typeset in 10.5/13pt Adobe Caslon Pro Regular by Fidus Design Pvt Ltd, Chandigarh.

Library of Congress Control Number: 2021942049

ISBN: 978-93-91370-97-8 (HB)

SAGE YODA Team: Amrita Dutta, Shipra Pant, Arpita Das, Ishita Gupta and Tanya Singh
Cover Design: Titash Sen

Contents

Acknowledgements   vii
Prologue: An Arrival and a Return   xi

1 What Is Suicide?   1

2 How Do We Engage with Suicidality?   39

3 Attempts at Engagement: Case Representations   69

4 Understanding Suicidality   127

Epilogue: Suicidality: A Relational Problem   153
Bibliography   161
About the Author   165
Index   167

Acknowledgements

The thoughts and reflections present in this work are a culmination of a long internal dialogue, not just in the duration of my training, but much before it and much after. To bring together multiple musings and preoccupations, in this form, would not be possible without many reliably present others who have lent themselves to engaging with my mind and compassionately making room for my feelings.

Professor Rachana Johri, thank you, first and foremost for always being *Ma'am*. From your excited curiosity about the questions I have asked, to your deep engagement with structures of thought. For allowing me to follow a thought through and building it with thinkers. For being patient but firm in my moments of doubt. Thank you for supporting me through unimaginable circumstances in gentle ways. Immense gratitude to you for your ways of teaching, your timely advice, and your presence.

Nupur Dhingra Paiva, thank you for bringing *Love and Rage* together. For teaching me the importance of bearing mixed feelings and building my capacity to tolerate my own. 2020 would have looked very different if it wasn't for you! Thank you for always making room for the many hats you wear but most of all, thank you for approaching me with self-belief and extending space for growth.

Arpita Das, thank you for recognizing the significance of this work, by just looking at an abstract! For your encouragement, patience and persistence in bringing it out, in this form. My research thesis would not have reached here, without you.

Padma Kasturi, your presence and kindness has allowed me to slowly return to my own thoughts, amidst the continuous chaos. Thank you for your nurturant listening, enabling me to write more affectively.

Neha Gupta and Shweta Dharamdasani, for your camaraderie, love and real talk. Thank you for being a great team and creating a sense of belonging to a team at Family Tree.

Closer home, I would like to thank my parents for providing me with a space to be creatively absorbed, but never isolated. Mom, thank you for patiently witnessing my writing process. For worrying about my internal deadlines and making me stick to a timeline. For lending your presence to my internal chaos by providing your own unique solutions. Dad, thank you for your constant enthusiasm about my work interests. For spending multiple hours listening to my writing. For being able to anticipate the next thought to develop. I'm truly grateful to both of you for all that you have done for me, and continue to do. I could never thank you enough for that.

To my family, thank you for being yourselves. For creating spaces for dialogue and disagreement across generations. For enabling me to know my truths, own them and live by them.

To my friends, I'd like to express my deepest love and gratitude for surviving this journey with me. Krishna S and Rhea Dubey, for carrying my work in your mind and being co-travellers in this journey. For making the time for multiple rantings and ravings and the many affect states this creates. Keya Khare and Aditi Sabharwal Mann, thank you for being a space to return to, outside and beyond this work. For excusing my absence, yet always being present to where I am at. For your warmth, comic relief, and your involvement. Suman Sahgal, thank you for always knowing. For your unwavering belief, love and care.

Raghav Sarin, where do I even begin? Thank you for tolerating the many things I have put you through, while never giving up on me. For always having faith in my abilities and standing by my choices. For looking out for me, in the long run, when I couldn't anticipate the next step. For being the custodian of my sanity. Thank you for always standing by me, rock solid.

Lastly, I would like to thank each of the happy inhabitants of my mother's garden. For being witness to the growth and evolution of this work. For teaching me the value of persistence and patience. For reminding me each day that growth is a slow process, sometimes not visible immediately. For truly letting me experience the power of slowing down and waiting—for it is only time and nurturance that lets the wild flowers bloom.

Prologue
An Arrival and a Return

An Arrival

To begin with, there was blankness, a sense of being in chaos and in flux. It began with the untimely loss of a friend. I've wondered about the timing of loss, whether that makes it easier. Perhaps age allows for a certain grace or explanation, while the nature of something untimely creates a flux. A flux that for me, pervaded the blankness. Thus, in the beginning, there was blankness. I was younger at the time, possibly more naïve. I cannot say I didn't see it coming, but when it came, it hit me in ways I couldn't anticipate. I never knew that it could come. For such is the nature of death; it interrupts.

She sent me a message that morning saying she didn't feel all that great, that I hadn't arrived and she thought she might die … this felt so adolescent to me and true to its nature, my adolescent self did not reply. That evening I got the news, she had jumped from the tenth floor. There was no note. Just conjecture of a possible difficulty with adjustment, of a difficult family history, of a transitional period that got interrupted. Something was lacking clearly, because why would someone so young, end up in a situation like this? So untimely. So much promise of what was still yet to come…. And yet she had tapped out on her own terms.

This was the first of a series of such events and each carried its own finger print. Each time it happened, it brought with it the difficulty of that which is untimely, difficult to explain, defies representation, and collapses meaning. To begin with, therefore, there was a symptom. A symptom I carried. A position I had been in, that made my subjectivity hypersensitive to the question of suicide. I had been constituted as both 'the witness' and 'the survivor'; both came with their own feelings and their own attempts at meaning. As I began to engage with that, it became a little easier to find representation. My master's thesis 'Naya Ayena: The Thanato Poetic Pleasure of Suicide' attempted to do just that. Taking up this research at that point in my life was a movement towards an avowal of meaning to events which had been largely disavowed, from my own psychic space and my immediate surroundings. That writing, for me, represented an avowal of the unformulated chaotic blankness and so began the preoccupation with understanding suicide.

The master's thesis gave me the opportunity to work with a young girl of 20 who attempted to take her life at the age of 13. My interaction with her allowed me to get a sense of the multiple things at play both within her and in her immediate environment. At the time I was inter-acting with her, she was at a different place in her life having moved away from her 13-year-old self, towards a self that had found both expression and meaning in her pursuit of art. In our work together we attempted to understand her (con)fused state of being at the age of 13, when she had attempted to take her life by swallowing a large amount of her prescription medication. She described herself as being in the midst of an *identity crisis* which spiralled into experimentation with drugs. Her sense of 'who' she is, was shaped by the diagnosis that she received when she was 12, which included bipolar disorder, Attention deficit hyperactivity disorder (ADHD), major depression and traits of borderlinity. Ours was an 11-month interaction in which I was drawn into many roles—the listener, the spectator, the friend, the ally and the tutor, while all the time also providing a space for engagement as she traversed through another transitional period towards admission to college. I felt like I had contained something, though she wasn't my patient and I wasn't a therapist, and the nature of the interaction carried only a novice understanding of what it meant to be both.

There are many things about the work I did with her, both in terms of my understanding of her and the construct of suicide itself, that became salient in my mind. Working with N allowed me to understand the importance of engagement. I imagined she would have been hesitant to talk about this part of her life, but on the contrary, she greeted me with excitement, as no one had ever asked her about this aspect of herself and that's what became important. I became aware of the multiple things I too carried in the moment, the fantasy of her shame, perhaps a sense of guilt at harming one's self—but here I had met someone who was excited about the prospect of a conversation around this.

A loss to suicide and an attempt at suicide are usually difficult to talk about. They carry within them many encrypted emotions that alter one's subjective position in ways that are, to some extent, foreseeable and yet, unique in their own way. The script of the psyche appears to be re-written around the untimely loss, or interruption, both of which feel deeply personal. Parallel to this, the process of mourning, which in itself is a long drawn out one, appears foreclosed by the notion of choice—a death by suicide becomes self-inflicted and a lot of time is spent in understanding what went wrong while covering up the attempt or the act. One can assume a social shame and a sense of guilt remains pervasive in understanding the loss. So, between an untimely loss and a death that seems chosen, mourning becomes a difficult process, especially in collective spaces. One is quick to find representation in a familiar language of deficit and pathology: there was an underlying depression, there was a financial strain, possibly a mental illness. While each one of these carries an element of what might have been the case, when I encountered these in discussions or read them in newspaper articles, something about them wouldn't address my concerns, leaving my questions unanswered. I wondered about the 'why' but gradually began to realize the impossibility of that question. The question of 'why' presents us with the inherent problem of representation and brings us face to face with the inherent unknowability of suicide. The representation allows for some meaning but not an answer, for the answer itself comes from an autopsy of a life that has passed. The 'why' remains impossible to decipher. I arrived here gradually and as I write this, my sense is, some work of mourning must have facilitated this shift such that I'm no longer in the grips of the 'why' anymore; some meaning has been found which, for now, seems enough.

As I progressed with my MPhil training, the thoughts and questions progressed and evolved with me. The question of suicide, how we understand it, how we work with it, what defines it and what constitutes it came to the forefront. The complexity of this question and the stance of the therapist is something that became of interest. I think the question of suicide also poses a fundamental question to our work in the clinic: how does psychotherapy traverse between a life in progress and the very real eventuality of death? How do we grapple with the life force and the death drive in the clinic? Where does it find an outlet?

In my own work with patients who have presented suicidal states, I have wondered what allows the transition from 'I've been thinking of taking my life' to 'these thoughts aren't coming as much anymore'. Where do these thoughts go? Are they predicated on a particular life historical circumstance and its change? Are they put aside only to resurface later? How do we mark a distinction between *suicidal ideation* and *suicidal intent,* and once again the question of 'what is this in service of?' comes to my mind. The stance of the therapist in moments like these become important in my understanding, not just for internal clarity, but in moments where one attempts to unravel these thoughts as one encounters difficult parts of the self and the other. Tolerating that is not in the least an easy task and it would be so much easier to take the moral angle of what you can do and what you can't; what is right and what is wrong about the question of suicide. What seems to be at play in this moment, is a sense of ambivalence on both sides; and withstanding *that* became the task in my understanding of this kind of work. To stay with the hyphenated space—open to exploring both sides.

In my own encounters, it is difficult to say something universal about suicide yet there remain affective resonances across each event. The play of despair and agency, of purpose and blankness, of something more that can be found beyond this life, appears to be a recurrent theme. What is most common, however, is that in each attempt, whether successful or unsuccessful, suicide creates a witness. An interesting witness, constituted not for the final account of the event, but for the life that has been, the life that has been lost, or the life that was attempting to be found. Suicide leaves behind a survivor that can be constituted in two ways—the self that survives the attempt at suicide or the other that is left behind, surviving the suicide of someone known to them. My clinical work has given me access to the former in a more nuanced manner. As for the latter, it remains a living position I occupy and inhabit.

Psychoanalysis as a frame, in many ways, became an important point of reference for me. As I have come to understand it, psycho-analysis doesn't take a moral stance on suicide as right or wrong, but endeavours to understand the multiple things at play in the *attempt* or the *desire* to end one's life. On the other hand, my training in psycho-social clinical studies and psychoanalytic psychotherapy shaped not just the clinician and researcher I am becoming, but also the subject position I have occupied as a student/trainee in a liberal arts university. In this process, there has been a deep reflection, not just on my auto-biographical experiences, but also on the social matrix that I began to occupy. Amidst my own struggles at identity formation, a psychosocial understanding of psychoanalytically informed work has become the playground for individual meditation in a collective space, where these questions have found home both in my mind and in my immediate environment.

My work in the public clinic has allowed me to interact with young adults between the ages of 17 to 25, some of whom were also students in the university. Simultaneously, being a student in the university exposed me to the different student movements that were taking place at the time. The university appears to have become a certain kind of space for students from different identities and locations. What kind of a space does the university become and how are these spaces negotiated with one's own location within a larger societal matrix? As I attempted to think about this, I also noted that over the last few years, there has been a steady increase in student suicides, especially in universities. Though there were many before, and many after, Rohith Vemula's suicide in Hyderabad University became an emblem-atic one.

Rohith was an aspiring, sensitively driven, politically oriented Ph.D. candidate in Hyderabad University who decided to take his life on 17 January 2016 after a suspension from the university. His letter became a point of revolution not just in student circles, but the larger political state as well. The letter left behind by Rohith became a signifier for the identity and caste struggles that have been plaguing university structures for a while. I still remember, when we got the news, what struck me most was the clubbing together of suicide as an event with caste. I don't think I had thought of them together prior to this point, making me only all too aware of the privileged position I occupy in the many social networks I inhabit. Caste also became a reality in my work in the public clinic, where I had the opportunity to witness struggles with identity and a re-writing of individual histories as one navigated the education one was being exposed to. With this in the backdrop, and my own location as a trainee in the university clinic, the epistemological questions around suicide gained significance—how would we tackle the spectre of suicide in a university space? What would be the ethics of care? And how would we understand the care of the self in these moments? These became important questions that further shaped the current work.

My research thus carries multiple layers and positions; at the level of the researcher's subjectivity, it moved from an autobiographical expression to the complexity of being a trainee in a public clinic. In this space, there has been a movement from understanding suicide to an exploration of *suicidality*. The shift came organically from working in the clinic and interacting with individuals who have communicated the presence of 'suicidal thoughts'. Even though on the referral form a common heuristic can be used to understand what we mean by suicidal thoughts, on further exploration it became apparent, in my work with such cases, that what we term 'suicidal' is not as neat as one would like it to be. Not all those who communicate such thoughts or intent make attempts of the same while there are some who communicate feeling better and proceed to make an attempt at taking their life. There are actions that could be understood as clearly self-destructive yet they wouldn't be classified as suicidal. Studying a tendency towards committing suicide then, is an attempt at understanding the complex interplay of the personal and the social in movements and communications of that tendency described as *suicidality*.

Keeping the above considerations in mind, the present work attempts to turn a psychosocial lens and further elaborate on how suicidality expresses itself in the space between the subject and the therapist. To expand on this, my research explored the multiple roles being navigated within the clinic as brought out in the transference dynamics between the subject and the therapist, the therapist and the institution of university, and the university in relation to the current socio-political constructions of our times. The roles that the therapist then occupies have not just been created through the individual life history of the therapist but are in relation to the life history of the subject that comes into the clinic, bringing with it each time its own location and tussle with identity, class, caste, and gender. The setting then, is never away from the larger social forces at play while working with an individual life history.

The space of the university and an attempt at psychoanalytically informed work in a clinic within the university are realities that I, as a trainee and a researcher, have had to grapple with and the attempt in this work is to reflect on the processing of this position. The larger question the work tried to engage with is the question of what kind of space the university is becoming in India today. The university in itself allows for a coming together of different sections of society, with different aspirations, histories, and marginalities. In parallel, it is alarming to note that the rate of death by suicide in the Dalit community is amongst the highest, a trend that cannot be reduced rather simply to just individual lack or distress.[1] Possibly, the 'bringing together of the identity crisis in an individual's life, with the contemporary crisis in historical development' (Erikson 1968) might allow us to understand the crisis further? Erikson's methodology of

---

[1] India has one of the world's highest suicide rates for youth aged 15 to 29, according to a 2012 *Lancet* report, which illustrated the need for urgent interventions for this demographic. (*The Lancet*, 23 June 2012).

bringing together the historical, the social, and the psychological could be useful in moving beyond the interiority of the subject of suicide (as psychotic/in breakdown/or deficit) towards also understanding the environment that constitutes this subjectivity.

Identity then could be an important link to understand what is structurally predicating this rise in the rate of death by suicide. Erikson indicates that, 'It is in adolescence that the ideological structure of the environment becomes essential for the ego, because without ideological simplification of the universe the adolescent ego cannot organize according to specific capacities and its expanding involvement' (Erikson 1968, p. 27). The question that begs to be answered then is: what is the ideological structure of the university being able to provide and not being able to provide to the student?

While engaging with these questions within the clinic, I also found myself becoming a part of student activities within the university. Having attended general body meetings, I began to realize and experience first-hand the different subject positions each person seemed to be coming from. What struck me the most in these moments was their identification through caste. It appeared as though a dialogue about the university as a structure, or the possible contents of what could be a representative constitution, could not commence without talking about caste. At moments, these junctures would not feel like the beginning of a dialogue but would become one group of people silencing another, predicated on a sense of historical violence. I wondered about this sense of violence and the marginality it created, both in its embodiment and its expression. The need for *psychological mindedness* while engaging with different positions of social otherness felt important to me at this point. How do I make room for a history of oppression that had been lived through these positions, while keeping the possibility of engagement open in the present? I found myself struggling at moments to keep conversation open, with care such that both dialogue and dissent did not only become violence. What compounded this further was the interaction between the student groups and the institution. Though at moments conversations around student concerns were possible, at other moments, the conversation would be completely derailed by what seemed like unthinking gestures on both sides. I say unthinking because of the nature of conflict; at any point one was always talking about a larger history, of a particular class privilege, a specific demand always hiding under it, a deeper need. Given the constraints on both sides coupled with an intensity of affect, miscommunication was imminent, leaving both parties feeling multiple things. At the level of the students what became a uniting factor was the sense of common cause, a fight for their rights. While at the level of the institution, there seemed to be a sense of hurt, at being portrayed as something they were not: oppressive deniers of rights. Caught between these two, I began to realize that there operated a strong fantasy of what it means to both teach and learn in a liberal arts university, especially one with the legacy of a name, such as ours[2].

Looking at each part individually, it wasn't difficult to get a sense of where both the student and the representative of institution were coming from, but in a collective meeting, it was difficult to get a sense of what each was becoming. Though a group analysis might help us here at this point, what struck me more was the collapse of engagement. Each group would shift to quick action: on one side, denial and dismissal while on the other, protest and campaign. There was no space for dialogue and as different as the representatives of the institution felt themselves from the students, what seemed most apparent was the pervasive sense of hurt on each end. As I wondered about these moments, it brought me back to the idea of psychological mindedness and psychological care. Unlike most other liberal arts

---

[2] Dr. B. R. Ambedkar University Delhi (Ambedkar University Delhi or AUD) is a public university with a multi campus, unitary structure with research, postgraduate and undergraduate programmes in the social sciences and the humanities. Mandated to focus on research and teaching in the social sciences and humanities and guided by Dr Ambedkar's vision of bridging equality and social justice with excellence, AUD considers it to be its mission to create sustainable and effective linkages between access to and success in higher education. AUD is committed to creating an institutional culture characterized by humanism, non-hierarchical and collegial environment, teamwork and nuturance of creativity. (https://aud.ac.in/about-us)

universities, ours had taken this term seriously and established a clinic[3] within the university space. I began to think how that space could be used to understand moments like these. It was one thing to have a student walk into the clinic and talk about the politics outside. But what seemed to be happening here was that as a trainee working within the clinic, I felt affected by the outside, drawn towards it and preoccupied with it. The interaction between the two became important in my mind, more so because the clinic existed spatially within the university. But how could the two come together to facilitate a support structure for the student that doesn't amount to moral policing and a breach of confidentiality? How does one facilitate a care of the self, while retaining a link to community?

In my two-year training in the university clinic, there were two parallel curiosities that continued to sustain themselves. First, the question of *suicide and suicidality;* and second, the question of the *interaction between the university and the clinic.* While working with students from the university, I noted that a large part of the work was around psychoeducation and enabling the students to use the space of the clinic in a way that could be facilitative for them. I noticed that with Bachelor's students, the expectation from the space was one of support and clarification, where they required active participation from the therapist. It seemed that listening to problems and providing support in the university structure proved more helpful than interpretative work. This often felt more like an extension of the idea

---

[3] Ehsaas is the Psychotherapy Clinic at Ambedkar University Delhi. It has been an initiative of the Centre of Psychotherapy and Clinical Research, School of Human Studies since 2011.

'At Ehsaas we work with a sliding fee scale and also offer psychotherapeutic support without charging any fee. This is done to ensure that all who need help can access it without feeling burdened by their economic constraints. Also, and equally important for us as a team of psychotherapists is establish a caring community. We believe that when people are respected and loved for who they are and are taken care of, eventually they themselves becoming caring and concerned human beings. In this respect, our low fee ethic is a response against the high commercialization in health care systems which is prevalent all around us today.' (https://aud.ac.in/ehsaas)

of mentorship, where the clinic would then function as a bridge between the world-view they came from and the world-view they were being exposed to. This isn't to say that the sense of crisis is any less, but I have found that in part addressing some of the issues has been more enabling to the work. It seemed that a sense of being a part of the university was being sought while simultaneously attributing authority to it, therefore distancing oneself from it—these were also subjects who usually referred to me as ma'am. With them it was difficult to go into larger life themes and the work remained around current distress and making the transition to a new environment. The work here was brief and as the sense of distress was alleviated, they would discontinue therapy, with the option of returning to it as and when required. In contrast to this, working with students of postgraduate studies had more potential for depth-oriented work, where exploration of life themes and impacts became a possibility. This, in my understanding, became an important differentiation between the training one was being given and the requirement of the subject that came in. Without accounting for the location of the clinic within the university space, it would have been difficult to adjust and respond to what was being differently sought by the subjects who entered the clinic.

Gradually, the corridor outside the clinic began to become more utilized by students. I have noticed many different moments and affect states during my walk to the clinic. I have often wondered about what makes it to the clinic and what doesn't but displays itself right outside it. My sense is that the socio-political matrix that constitutes the university has an important bearing on what does and doesn't come to the clinic, the individual filling in the referral-form being a microcosm of a tussle between self-care and the world-view the student comes from, i.e., community. Though there is curiosity about the clinic within the university, vocal students who make their presence felt within student groups, usually don't come to the clinic, or they come for a few sessions and then discontinue. It seems that a sense of being in a community or group is also able to provide something that acts as a scaffold for identity formation. A sense of psychological care then is not limited to seeking an appointment in the clinic but also finds spaces in collectives and movements outside it, where there is a strong sense of community. As long as a sense of community is retained, there seems to be containment but it would also be important to think about what this sense of community becomes symbolic of, what does it contain and what its collapse could mean, especially for an individual.

Amid these preoccupations, I encountered another sense of interruption. As I gathered data for my research, of cases that display a tendency towards suicide and its interaction within the clinic space, I also found myself preoccupied with suicide as an event in a university space. Its nature of impact, its signification, the kind of processing it would require on multiple levels and the need to have thought around it, became important to the trainee in me, the trainee who always remained close to the subject position of being a student in the university. These questions found space in the process of my training where I began to wonder about protocols and procedures while working with difficult states. The nature of the scaffolding and support structure for the therapist became important in my mind. As I voiced these concerns, I was met with multiple responses and at moments it was difficult to not feel these personally. As I found, thinking about and engaging with suicide and suicidality carries within it its own inherent difficulty.

Coupled with the interaction of the multiple subject positions that I too have carried, of a life history, the position of a trainee and a student would make these moments all the more complex. There seemed to be multiple anxieties I was constantly aware of and multiple domains that remained unthinkable. There remained too many questions that were difficult to narrow down, interconnected in my mind as they remained. I wonder if that too tells us something about the construct one is attempting to look at in this work: not lending itself to easy resolution and signification, for there still remains so much to be thought through. This need to *think through* presented itself to me like an urgency, from what I would hear in the clinic, to what I would experience in the university as a space. Something about this thinking through felt urgent, at moments anxiously so.

It is around this time that the news came: a young 19-year-old had taken his life, a second-year undergraduate student who had been an active part of the university as a space. It is difficult to convey what that moment felt like, when I received this news. I felt blank; though it wasn't an unfamiliar blankness, yet there was something different about it this time. What made the moment harder was that this young person was someone I had worked with in the clinic. My work with him was brief support work which had terminated over two months before this moment. P was one of those students who I felt had navigated both the clinic and the student communities. My work with him had been a part of discussions about the thesis due to his subject position within the university space, the two worlds he was trying to bring together and his attempts at identity formation as he traversed multiple locations within the university, along with being a subject in the clinic. Until then, I hadn't considered him 'high risk', as he had communicated feeling better to me but had terminated the sessions with the option to come back when needed. An option he *had*, clearly and explicitly. An option I continue to wish he had taken.

My first impulse was to go back to my notes (I felt so glad to have those notes!) to trace if there was something that I had missed. Was there something I could have done? What had happened? Why hadn't he just called! There were so many questions, and in those questions, a sense of history that I had carried of P, of the work we had done, of our interaction, began to get blurry. As the shock of this event hit me, the first thing I felt the need to do was cling to memory. As I battled my own sense of internal chaos, my case notes helped in returning to the work that we had done together and to recollect the position P was in. But how did he get there? Why? What had precipitated it? The notes could not yield these answers. I'm not sure if those are the right questions either. The nature of this work would say that they aren't; but post the interruption, the event restructured memory, almost robbing it of meaning, casting me once more in the light I had known before, of an impact that felt familiar, or rather a loss that didn't feel unfamiliar. But this was different; here I wasn't the friend or the family member, I was the therapist.

Where does one even begin to mourn? In that moment, I felt a dual loss: as a student who has shared public spaces and dialogues, as well as the therapist who had worked with him in the clinic. This young person was in the midst of developing a sense of self as a first-generation member of his family to get an education. He carried on his shoulders a hypersensitive awareness of being in this world, with the promise of being more and doing more. As I recall this particular fact more than why he chose to take his life, I feel drawn to the quest of finding a representation for precisely this: the impact of P's life on those around him, including our work together; what could we have done better or differently? Not 'why did he do this?' But what can we do better, what might we open ourselves to and how do we engage with this? Between an individual life history and its interaction with a structure like the university, what kind of scaffold would one need to think about in the process of identity formation and development? This became a point to return to, again and again, in my mind.

Prior to P's death, there had been questions around the possibility of such a scenario in my mind; reading about the rising rates, following the trends on universities would often make me think about how one would mourn a loss in the student community if one ever got there? Before this work could have followed its hypothetical trajectory, I found myself at that juncture. The question remains, how do we begin to mourn this loss? My research work came back to this moment as a point of reflection, as an avenue for signification of a mourning that remains undesignated, and a blankness that attempted to find a representation.

2020: A Return

At the turn of the new decade, we found ourselves in the middle of a pandemic, unable to imagine the light at the end of the tunnel. 2020 was spent moving between the new normal and the hope that some amount of normalcy would return, from a forgotten version of the world, sooner rather than later. In all this, we forgot once more that the version of the world we inhabited before, did have a fair share of unaddressed problems. Concerns. Symptoms of what we were going through. One of them, which continues to go unaddressed is the rising rates of suicide. Except now, in the middle of the pandemic, mental health is becoming a growing concern.

As an early career psychotherapist, there has never been a doubt in my mind that human beings are resilient. So resilient that at times our desire to hold on to a sense of external coherence can result in ignoring, neglecting and dismissing our internal preoccupations. Our focus on moving forward sometimes comes at the cost of neglecting the internal struggle that comes with it. Developmentally, as we move from being children to adolescents to adults, each stage brings with itself its own crisis. At the same time, in any given historical moment, there will be forces of socio-political change that will determine the nature of our environment. War, political upheaval, pandemics and such like will decide what social locations and positions are made available for individual and collective growth. To understand the rising rates of suicide in India then, it becomes imperative to engage with the context and location of the individual, while keeping in mind that the individual doesn't exist in isolation but is always in *relation to* Others—significant others, family, community, a larger collective.

This rise in suicide rates is not caused by the pandemic. The past 10 years have witnessed a steady increase in suicide rates across the globe, and particularly, in India. The *Lancet Report* (2012) stated that India has one of the world's highest suicide rates for youth aged 15 to 29 (para 4). In a report filled by the Indian National Crime Record Bureau (2014), it was noted that this increase appeared to be the highest amongst minority populations, especially amongst Dalits and Muslims. This was also the first report that attempted to create a record, not just based on basic demographics and gender, but caste and religion as well.

In January 2020, *The Hindu* reported '...every hour one student commits suicide in India, with about 28 such suicides reported every day, according to data compiled by the National Crime Records Bureau (NCRB). The NCRB data shows that 10,159 students died by suicide, an increase from 9,905 in 2017, and 9,478 in 2016'

(Garai 2020). In September 2020, *India Today* added, 'more than 1.39 lakh Indians died by suicide in the year 2019, 67 per cent of which were young adults (18–45 years), shows the latest data released by the National Crime Records Bureau.'

> Of the total 1.39 lakh suicides recorded in the year 2019, roughly 93,016 or 67 per cent were committed by youngsters (aged 18+ and below 45). Of these, 31,725 (34 per cent) suicides happened because of family problems, marriage related issues drove 7,293 (7.3 per cent) people to suicide. Mental illness was a cause of suicide for 6,491 people or 7 per cent of the total suicide committed by youngsters. Drug abuse/alcoholic addiction drove 5,257 (5.6 per cent) to die by suicide and love affairs drove 4,919 (5.2 per cent) people to kill themselves (Rampal 2020).

These trends are alarming but what remains a greater cause for alarm is the manner in which we treat this information. On 14 June 2020 when Sushant Singh Rajput died by suicide, every news channel, every household, every WhatsApp group was overflowing with conspiracies and theories on what led this young actor to take such an unfortunate step. What could have been an opening to address India's growing mental health crisis turned into everything else but that. As the media trial moved between suicide and murder, drugs and the Bollywood nexus, mental illness or financial distress, what remained out of focus was a very simple fact—all the theories aside, no one would ever know what happened. This was post facto.

Death by suicide presents us with the inherent problem of the 'unknown'. It interrupts the way we make meaning. Interruptions are uncomfortable because they create a forced pause. In this pause we have a choice: to follow causal meaning-making or to engage with what emerges from this unknown. The former is the quicker option: cause effect meaning. The latter, however requires us to open ourselves up to our own internal world and the feelings it brings. 'The apparent reasons being reported for Sushant Singh's alleged suicide are no less than what an ordinary person committing suicide would face otherwise.' (Rampal 2020). There was nothing 'special' about this except for his public location and historical timing. Thus, it became news. There have been many before, there will be many after. And until we find ways to engage with our internal world and its relation to our collective distress, these statistics will continue to grow with each report and yet nothing much will change.

Understanding the nature of suicidality among the youth in India has been a problem in my mind for over a decade. As I trained to become a psychotherapist, every research opportunity became an entry point into engaging with this preoccupation. In the last two years as I reflected on what my research findings were, I began to realize that our misconceptions about suicide as an act dominate our engagement with people who feel suicidal. The spaces for active, non-judgemental engagement remain limited. There is something inherently terrifying about being faced with that level of distress. I can now say this with no uncertainty as a trained professional. Can we make room for this distress as family members, friends, significant others and colleagues?

If we don't acknowledge how terrifying this engagement with internal distress can be, we will not be able to make room for those moments of suicidality that creep up on us. In denying our distress, we neglect the impact these communications make, reinforcing the suicidal person's world-view: that they do not impact, they are alone, their life means nothing. The truth is that if someone wants to take their life, they don't need to talk about it. Nothing can truly come between that decision and action, if the individual has willed it. But, if there is an attempt at engagement, are we prepared to make space for it?

This book is one such attempt. In the course of my training as a psychotherapist, my MPhil research attempted to understand psychosocial representations of suicidality in a university clinic. With the help of two case studies, my research attempted to elaborate on that which is being termed as *suicidality*, and the way it presents itself and communicates itself within the clinic. It also explored the various roles and dynamics between the subject and the therapist in an attempt to give the reader a sense of the *nature* of work, its anxieties, its difficulties, and its strengths.

As I return to this thesis two years later, there are many things I would do differently and yet there are some things I would insist on repeating. So, this is partially an autobiographical account of what it has been like to work with suicidality at close quarters in particular settings. At the same time, it is an endeavour to make accessible the complexity of suicidality and its expressions. The hope, while putting this out there, remains that through this process, a possibility of how to engage emerges, because even if suicide gets typecast as an individual act of free will, *suicidality* is a communication of a relational problem.

CHAPTER 1

What Is Suicide?

Conceptual Review: Setting Up a Framework

In my work within the university clinic, I observed a dialectic between suicide as an act and suicidality as a tendency. The tendency before the act, and its representations and communications form a large part of the data, which however cannot be understood without reflecting on the nature of the act itself and what it has come to symbolize in this particular space. The conceptual review thus begins by tracing the connotation of suicide in a diagnostic framework. Through this, it will engage with the use of these frameworks while working with the suicidal subject, within the particularity of the milieu that they are placed in.

Suicide: The Problem of Definition

As I have mentioned in the Prologue to the book, the present research question originated with a curiosity about the construct of suicide. The *Oxford English Dictionary* defines suicide as 'the action of killing oneself'. In the psychiatric framework, suicide (both in the form of an attempt or a preoccupation) is given an interesting position. Though neither the International Classification of Diseases (ICD) compiled by the World Health Organisation (1979) nor the Diagnostic and Statistical Manual (DSM) formulated by the American Psychiatric

Association give it the status of an individual disorder, being suicidal or having a 'suicidal ideation'[1] occurs as a comorbidity with a host of disorders such as bipolarity, depression, mania, schizophrenia and substance abuse, to name a few. In the latest addition of the DSM (V) a new disorder termed 'suicidal behaviour disorder'[2] has been added, which seems to be a response to the increase in suicide rates across the globe. In the evolution of diagnosis, it appears that suicide is moving from a preoccupation of thoughts, towards a manifest behaviour. In this diagnostic system, it is the manifested behaviour that can be considered a disorder. Could this movement imply better control over the rise in suicides?

Alvarez (1999) in his book *Savage God*, elaborated that we, as human beings, need to construct fallacies around the manifestation of the act of suicide. It is as if, 'suicide is rejected because s/he is so completely rejecting' (1999, p. 166). The fallacies have been conceptualized

---

[1] ICD 9 defines <u>suicidal ideation</u> as 'concerns thoughts about or an unusual preoccupation with suicide. The range of suicidal ideation varies greatly from fleeting thoughts, to extensive thoughts, to detailed planning, role playing (e.g. standing on a chair with a noose), and incomplete attempts, which may be deliberately constructed to not complete or to be discovered, or may be fully intended to result in death, but the individual survives (e.g., in the case of hanging in which the cord breaks) (ICD 9, 1979. code: V62.84).

[2] The DSM V recently created a new diagnosis termed <u>Suicidal Behaviour Disorder</u>. The diagnosis is premised on 'five criterions [sic] with two specifiers':

1. The individual has made a suicide attempt within the past two years.
2. The criterion for non-suicidal self-injurious behaviour is not met during the aforementioned suicide attempts.
3. The diagnosis is not applied to preparation for a suicide attempt, or suicidal ideation.
4. The act was not attempted during an altered mental state, such as delirium or "confusion".
5. The act was not ideologically motivated, e.g., religious or political.

Other specifiers are:

Current: Not more than 12–24 months since last attempt.
In Remission: More than 24 months since last attempt (American Psychiatric Association, 2013).

in such a way that they are likely to appeal to the rational individual. He states that the need to believe in the accidentality of death is so strong that these fallacies go unquestioned on many occasions. The fallacies include: Suicide is a cry for help; it is an act of great passion; it is a product of bad weather; it can be considered a national habit; those who threaten it will not kill themselves; and, those who have attempted it, will not try again.

The last two are the most dangerous fallacies to be operating with. To assume that those that threaten suicide will not kill themselves or those who have attempted it will not try it again, invites a passive stance in engaging with suicidality. Despite the fact that these fallacies have been proved wrong on countless occasions through rational logic, evidence and statistics, one still employs them in an attempt to understand the suddenness of the death, because they reduce the complexity of the construction of suicide and 'reduce the suicide's anguish to hysterical self-pity, to an attention seeking device- jejune, ostentatious, disproportionate' (Alvarez 1999, p. 166). It appears that through these fallacies, one is able to retain a significant distance from the subject who chooses suicide as though there is nothing much else to consider, as if the reasons for ending one's life are obvious. It allows one to hold on to an assimilable explanation, which we appear to be unwilling to let go of, especially when it comes to suicide. I often wonder whether the movement of suicide, from a preoccupation of thoughts, to a manifest behaviour within the diagnostic frame, could also be a re-enactment of the fallacies around suicide, making regulation and prediction a possibility.

There has been a steady increase in suicides and suicide rates in India since 2014. In the same year, World Health Organization (4 September 2014) filed a report which noted that India not only had a steadily increasing rate of suicides but also had the highest number of suicides in the year 2012 in the South Asian region (para. 3). These rates have continued to increase in the following years. *Hindustan Times* (2017) alerts us that, 'India has one of the world's highest suicide rates for youth aged 15 to 29, according to a Lancet report of 2012, which illustrated the need for urgent interventions for this demographic' (para. 4). In 2014, for the first time, the National Crime Records Bureau in India was asked to collect data on suicides based on religious and caste groups. This was a new exercise, given that these records are usually demarcated by basic demographics such as urban/rural, male/female and age. According to *The Indian Express* (2016) the reports have still not been published as they imply an epidemic increase in suicide rates in minority populations, specifically Muslims and Dalits (para. 3). In a legislative move to address mental health concerns, the Mental Health Care Bill was introduced in the Parliament in 2013, which further became an act in 2016. The act decriminalizes suicide, which had been considered a criminal offence according to Section 309 of the Indian Penal Code until recently. Interestingly, the bill proposes a largely biomedical model of diagnosis and care that does not repeal Section 309 but specifically adds the presumption of 'mental illness' (unless proved otherwise) as a determinant of the event. This determinant forecloses the possibility of the act of suicide being a communication of anything other than mental distress. Given that the rise in suicides is most prevalent, and not limited to Farmer, Dalit and Academic suicides, one wonders, who does this presumption of mental illness serve? What does it imply? What is it a symptom of?

Law, Culture, Society: Implications of What Constitutes Suicide

As I reviewed further, I noticed an interaction between law and culture, where transitions in the cultural fabric appeared to be marked by transitions in the legal sphere. The amendment of Section 309 decriminalizing suicide seems to be a representation of the same. A similar pattern where a cultural practice remoulds itself around new formed legalities, has been noted by other thinkers as well.

Ashis Nandy (1999) in his article 'Sati: A Ninetieth Century Tale of Women, Violence and Protest' traced the decline and rise of sati as a response to larger cultural changes. He posited that from the rise of sati to its criminalization, there were cultural ambivalences being negotiated. It became symptomatic of the tussle between what is considered indigenous and that which is imported; between the Brahmanical and the folk. The imported value system insisted on a criminalization of sati, while the Brahmanical felt this would change the cultural fabric in India. In understanding this, Nandy (1999) infers that, 'social change then comes to mean not only changes in rites, rituals and practices but also a changed relationship between cultural symbols and individual motives' (p. 305). One is led to query then, what does the rise in suicide rates and the decriminalization of suicide represent for our cultural psyche? What kind of ambivalences are being navigated in the majorities' relationship with the minorities such that suicide is becoming an option?

To further understand the interaction between law and culture, a reflection on the nature of the social, in which these transitions take place, also becomes significant. In other words, to understand the rise in suicide rates, the decriminalization of suicide and its implications in particular, an understanding of suicide which is not just limited to the psychological is vital.

Durkheim in his seminal work on *Suicide* (1897), offered a direction to understand this relationship with social change and fluctuations in rates. In choosing suicide as an object of enquiry, he attempted to prove through opposition that in an event where one thinks they are most free is precisely the moment when they are most governed by society. He specifically chose suicide as his object of enquiry because it is considered an individual psychological act of free will. In the formulation of his larger theory, Durkheim believed that if he managed to show the play of collective consciousness in an act that is considered so deeply psychological, then he would succeed in making a case for the external, constraining and general impact of the social fact. While understanding Durkheim today, our attention is drawn to social factors that play a role in the complexity of an act that is considered so deeply individualistic.

Through Durkheim (1897), one notes how the individual is a product of society. He theorizes that an external, constraining, general fact has to exist for a group or a society to exist in *solidarity*. There is a shift from what he called *mechanical solidarity* to *organic solidarity* which results in the emergence of the individual. The shift happens because competition for resources is reduced by making a movement from independence to interdependence. The individual, according to Durkheim, is not a reality until this shift in society takes place. Organic solidarity is then the glue that holds society together, but this solidarity may itself possess a pathological character.

Durkheim in some respects situated suicide as the problem of modernity. He attempted to understand how the individual is impacted in times of dramatic social change, and how these changes impact the individual and the group, making some more susceptible to suicide than others. In his theory he postulated a typology of suicide based on two axes: *integration* which referred to 'the sense of belonging and inclusion, love, care, and concern that can flow (or not flow) from social ties' (Wray, Colen, Pescodolido 2011, p. 507); and *regulation*, which was the 'monitoring, oversight and guidance that come from social ties' (Ibid., p. 508). The integration axis, furthermore contained *Egoistic Suicide* on one side and *Altruistic Suicide* on the other. Egoistic Suicide is caused by the fact that the individual is not well integrated within society. There is an emphasis on 'I-ness', and these types of suicides happen in a quiet corner because the individual is unable to rely on social bonds to overcome the problem. Altruistic Suicide occurs when the individual is so rigidly integrated into society that it results in a negative kind of suicide. Sati would be an example of this kind of suicide because the identity of the widow is so structured by society that the idea to protest or to even think of saying 'no' does not cross the individual's mind because they are that deeply integrated in the group.

On one side of the regulation axis, there is *Anomic Suicide*. Through this, Durkheim undertook the question of modernity. In modernity as a whole, the suicide rates go up as there is a breakdown of norms with the replacement of mechanical solidarity with organic solidarity and the creation of an individual. In this chaotic environment, the individual ends up asking more from society than the latter is capable of offering. The Anomic Suicide happens when the moral hold that the collective consciousness used to have on the individual weakens.

In contrast, the *Fatalistic Suicide* is a result of too much regulation of the individual by the collective consciousness.

Durkheim's thesis does not imply that individual suicides should be explained in this manner. He is instead alerting us to the idea that even if there are psychological predispositions towards suicide, the committing of the act will be a result of precipitating social factors. This implies a fluctuation such that, if there is an increase or decrease in the integration or the regulation axis, the risk of suicide will be greater. 'Only when these forces are balanced, when the individual feels at harmony with their own needs and the demands of the group, does the suicide rate diminish' (Wray et al. 2011, p. 509). One can wonder then, what would the applicability of Durkheim's classification in the current scenario be? The increasing rate of suicides and the decriminalization of suicide are both symptomatic of the times that we live in. They attempt to bring something larger than just the individual act into dialogue, and it would be important to consider the social factors at play in these moments.

In a critique of Durkheim's typology, Douglas (1967) emphasised the need to recognize cultural and social meanings attributed to suicide, which have an important bearing on what gets recorded as suicide and what does not. Douglas further points out that Durkheim's typology 'failed to consider suicide as a meaningful social action under-taken by individuals and failed likewise to attend to the variation in definitions of suicide observable among those who were charged to determine if a suicide had occurred' (Wray et al. 2011, p. 509). This would also have important implications for the trends and demographics regarding suicide, in the way they are presented and what they represent in a particular context. It is important to note that not every kind of self-chosen death is termed as a suicide, and there seems to be a distinction between suicide as a form of protest (as seen in self immolations), suicide as a weapon (the suicide bomber) and suicide as sacrifice (for example in the act of sati). From the onset, there seems to be a particularity that is ascribed to what is finally termed as suicide. The explanations of this ascription seem to be linked to a kind of deficit—either mental, economic or social. The interplay of multiple forces that come together in the formation of such an act is difficult to stay with as one moves towards a unilateral understanding of the person who choses suicide, which renders suicide more of an individualistic act determined by between either agency or deficiency. Though in reality, the act is located somewhere between agency and a sense of deficit, further highlighting the difficulty in defining it.

Taking a cue from Douglas (1967), it becomes important to understand what is being termed as suicide in the present Indian context. It is difficult to trace a genealogy of this term specific to the Indian cultural context. Here, there is a distinction between *atmhatya/khud khushi* and the idea of *praan tyaagna/iccha mrityu.* Interestingly, the former translates into suicide and the latter translates into euthanasia. This evokes a mythic understanding, which takes us closer to a sense of surrender, sacrifice, honour and duty such that the word suicide would not be attributed to an action (like a son bartering his life for the father or a daughter retuning to mother earth by will) but attributed more to a sense of surrender than an active giving up/or taking life. Perhaps this implies a cultural ambivalence between life and death, or a fluidity between these positions. Though these questions remain outside the scope of the present study, they form important junctures in highlighting the difficulty of understanding the concept of suicide from the point of view of definition.

Thinking of Durkheim's typology along with Douglas's correction might be helpful in understanding the rise in suicide rates. It seems, in the present Indian context, reports of an increase in suicide rates are going unpublished, and in particular minority groups are seeing a rise in suicide rates and a new constellation of these significations are appearing in the university as a setting. After Rohith Vemula's death by suicide, it becomes important to reflect on what kind of a space the university is becoming and the nature of the position it occupies when a student commits suicide. Given the difficulty in tracing genealogy and the fluidity of concepts around life and death in our culture, how do we understand *this* movement of suicide and its signification? Does it represent a disequilibrium in the integration and regulation axis? What could this tell us about our social constellations at this point?

University as a Site

It must be said at the outset that the university became a significant site to understand suicide not just because of the rise in the rates of death by suicide, but also owing to my location of being a university student and trainee in a university clinic. It must also be said at this point that while thinking about the rise of suicide rates among the youth, it becomes important for us to think about the nature of the crisis that is being negotiated by this population in the spaces they inhabit and engage with. Developmentally, it becomes important to think about the needs and subject positions being navigated in these life histories. The university allows for different sections of society to come together with different aspirations, histories and marginalities. However, the setting of the university also locates itself within an urban environment, while making itself accessible to those outside it. It represents a structure that makes a movement between tradition and modernity possible, while also providing a reflection on one's own subject positions, especially if it is a liberal arts university. It offers the possibilities of new identity formations based on the navigation of transitions and conflicts, providing a playground for the subject's internal world to come in contact with the external world order. In that sense, the university becomes instrumental in the navigation between the inside and outside of not just the space the subject is coming from, but structures of group, family and socio-economic location as well. As a sense of self develops, a sense of what is other *than* the self and other *to* the self also gets demarcated in these moments. Both inclusion and marginalization become apparent as multiple subject positions that are made available through critical reflection and engagement. From a language of communication and pedagogy of education, to an ethic of care of the self and the other, the university exposes the subject to a sense of crisis: 'a loss of personal sameness and historical continuity' (Erikson, 1968, p. 16).

As I observed these transitions, both as someone working in the university clinic and as someone who has been a part of the university as a student, I noted that there seemed to be a gap—between a need experienced by the student, and the expectation of how these needs should be met by the institution. A gap that would at some moments result in protest or in a complete breakdown of communication. Between feeling integrated into the university space and being regulated by it, a moment of crisis seemed to present itself, highlighting the cultural ambivalences both the students and the institution seemed to be negotiating. Identity locations on both ends appeared to be in opposition to each other, which in themselves require a separate reflection. It is possibly in moments like these that Rohith Vemula's suicide becomes an important signifier of the struggles in the university space.

Rohith was an aspiring, sensitively driven, politically oriented PhD candidate in Hyderabad University who decided to take his life on 17th January 2016 after a suspension from the university. His letter became a point of revolution not just in student circles, but the larger political state as well. The suicide letter left behind by Rohith Vemula became a signifier for identity and caste struggles that have been plaguing the university structures for a while. It not only highlighted a failure at an institutional level, but a social crisis of faith and care. It is important to note that Rohith was not the first suicide that had taken place in a university space (and his was certainly not the last). An article in the *Hindustan Times* (2016), cautioned that though his death has drawn the country's attention to the University of Hyderabad, 'suicides among Dalit students here is not a new phenomenon' (para. 1). Rohith was the sixth victim within the university itself. With Rohith Vemula's suicide, however, the question of discrimination and marginalization within the university setting became important to think about further, bringing the structural problem of caste into discourse.

The headline of an article published in *The Wire* (2017) cautions that 'India's Universities Are Falling Terribly Short on Addressing Caste Discrimination'. According to the article,

> The prevalence of caste-based discrimination in Indian universities has been an open secret for decades. While some Dalit student suicides have been more widely reported in recent years, away from the headlines, direct and indirect systemic discrimination continues to suffocate the lives and thwart the education of Dalit students across the country.

In some cases, an apathetic indifference may be seen on the part of the administration to the social and economic margins that some students come from. Coupled with the absence of a caste consciousness, further marginalization takes place in some cases, either consciously, by occupying an 'anti' role or unconsciously, due to the presumption of being 'non-casteist'. At a structural level, although there seem to be mandates and remedial actions stated by the University Grants Commission, their implementation has been difficult in a majority of universities, either due to lack of funding or for reasons not specified (*The Wire* 2017, para. 3). The pressure seems to be building however in moments of organized student politics, which in some cases has garnered active faculty support. There remains a continuous interplay of hope and dread in these moments. Though a systemic change cannot occur overnight, continuous engagement and reflection is an important step in the right direction. Harsh Mander (2017), while mourning Rohith Vemula, wrote,

> …can we at least ensure that classrooms, schools and universities become places where children and young people are valued for what they are, for the qualities of their hearts and heads, for their efforts as much as their failures, and not for the accident—fatal or otherwise—of their birth? (para. 77).

With this backdrop, the epistemological questions around suicide gained significance in this work. Does Rohith become a signifier around which the question of suicide in the university space can be reorganized? And following this, how is the spectre of suicide in moments of crisis, within the space of the university, addressed? Johri (2017) aptly stated, 'Rohith's death has brought the question of caste to the centre of concern in the sphere of higher education. These questions pose difficult issues including those of epistemology, the validity of epistemological claims that disregard the question of caste.' Though these questions do not lend themselves to easy signification or answers, they define closely the field within which the present study is located.

In understanding suicide as not just an individual act of impaired judgement but rather as dominated by socio-cultural-politico factors, a few of which may lie well within the realm of awareness, a different relationship to agency, surrender and mutuality could come to light which may further enable us to engage suicide and understand how to work with it in this context.

Clinic within the University: Psychoanalysis and Suicide

To establish a clinic within the university space, given the present situation, seems to be an important requirement. However, this also creates an interesting subject position and would invite a host of fantasies about the clinic: of surveillance; of the coexistence of community and self-care; of curiosity and intrigue; and possibly of scaffolding through transition. After the Mental Health Care Bill and decriminalization of suicide, the understanding of suicide becomes particular to mental illness which is defined as 'a substantial disorder of thinking, mood, perception orientation or memory that grossly impairs judgment, behaviour, capacity to recognize reality or ability to meet the ordinary demands of life, mental conditions associated with the abuse of alcohol and drugs.' In the wake of Rohith Vemula's suicide, the discourse around the university underwent a shift, where caste and marginality became highlighted as important structural constraints on collective growth. Given these two moments, how does one understand a preoccupation with suicide or suicidal thoughts in a clinic that is located within the university? What are the necessary considerations, revisions or additions that would be required in the clinicians' understanding, while working within a clinical space with its own pedagogy and location while interacting with the reconstructed space of the university in the present socio-political scenario?

Keeping in mind the prevalent socio-economic realities, the clinic I trained in offers low fee psychotherapy services informed by a psychosocial approach to psychoanalytic psychotherapy. Unlike psychiatry, psychoanalysis attempts to look at suicide beyond the dyad of the normal and abnormal. It attempts to bring into dialogue the internal forces at play in the act and in the attempt. Here, suicide is understood as an *affect deluge, a psychotic fantasy,* where there is an assumption that a part of the self will survive and the attempt will not end in death. There is a particular kind of Other being constructed in this hypothesis, one who is somewhat not connected to reality, and slowly slipping into the realm of the psychotic.

John Maltsberger (2004), in his paper, 'Descent into Suicide', elaborated that the descent into suicide is precipitated by affect deluge[3]. Through an inability to master this affect deluge, the eventual suicide is not so much a self-destruction as much as it is a self-defence. Can it be posited that there is a protective function being executed by the suicidal self that may show an attempt to preserve something (even though it remains deluded)? This postulation initially provided the work with a structure through which I could understand the creation of the suicidal subject as a process of an external event that creates impacts in the internal reality. It is predicated on the fact that there is something overwhelming in the environment which acts as a trigger of some sort. Maltsberger's paper (2004, p.657) postulated that the act of committing suicide is a result of experiencing the body as persecutory and there is a delusion of grandiosity which lets the individual believe that they are preserving something by killing themselves. This paper also gave rise to the possibility that there is a fantasized preservation of some part of the self in the movement towards death. What, however, is the nature of this part of the self that is being preserved in a suicide?

In my understanding, this part of the self is close to Winnicott's (1960) construction of the *True Self.* The True Self is the self from which the spontaneous and creative gestures come. It is the instinctual part of the self in which moments of aliveness are rooted. The False Self, on the other hand, is created in an environ-ment in which the instinctual part of the self has not been allowed to

---

[3] The aspect of 'Affect Deluge' is the first stage of 'suicidal collapse' (p. 653) postulated by Maltsberger (2004) which 'can be compared to flooding, finds the patient awash in an overwhelming deluge of intolerable painful feeling'.

develop due to failures in the environment. This self is born out of compliance and 'finds a way of enabling the True Self to live' (ibid., p.147).

In a movement that leans towards health, if the False Self cannot create conditions for the True Self to come into its own, 'there must be recognized a new defence against exploitation of the True Self, and if there is doubt then the clinical result is suicide' (ibid., p. 142). In this movement towards death, there is an imagination of preserving what is True to the self of self. Can this movement then still be considered pathological? Winnicott, in his postulations, has not implied whether the constructions of the True Self and False Self in themselves are pathological, but instead pointed to the nature of the environment that results in the construction of the False Self and how this same environment affects the interaction between the two. Winnicott postulated that the False Self's desire to annihilate the Real Self is an attempt to preserve the True Self. This in his understanding, represents a movement towards psychic health. In doing so, I feel that he put into question the idea of the pathology of suicide in the psychoanalytical framework. For the present work, an important point of reflection would also become, how we engage with the true self, psychosocially, and further thinking about whether true self gestures are granted more easily in some cases than others.

Karl Menninger (1933) in his paper, 'Psychoanalytic Aspects of Suicide', indicated that suicide is born out of a triad between three wishes: the wish to kill, the wish to be killed, and the wish to die. The suicidal wish is situated at the crossroads of these three wishes. The wish to kill represents the oscillation between constructive and destructive forces, and can also be considered to be a wish to eat the other (Lewin 1950, p. 89). The wish to be killed is an inaction of submissive forces and can also be seen as the wish to be eaten. The wish to die can be considered the wish to sleep. The paradox of this wish to die is that the person 'who has wished to kill himself, does not wish to die'. This wish to die may be only 'another disguise for the frequently observed phenomena commonly interpreted as birth fantasies or more accurately, a desire to return to the womb'

(Menninger 1933, p. 90). This fantasy of return to a prior state has been documented by other psychoanalysts as well, particularly while understanding the fantasies around suicide as an act, while also under-scoring the nature of psychosis within the subject.

Schachter (1999) stated that a suicidal state of mind is predicated upon 'an inability to negotiate a secure sense of separateness within which a coherent self can develop' (p. 123). It can also be 'seen as failed mourning of the infantile relationship with the mother which leads to a profound sense of emptiness and despair' (ibid., p. 124). In this state of mind, there appears to be a pre-oedipal stuck-ness, such that a coherent separate sense of self and other has not been established. This stuck-ness can be understood further by looking at Glasser's concept of the *core complex* (1992).

> In the core complex, the fantasy of fusion with the idealized mother is envisaged as the means of meeting the desire for complete safety and security. The mother however is a split figure. She is conceived as both engulfing and indifferent. The consequent annihilation anxiety provokes two concurrent defensive responses: narcissistic withdrawal and aggression with the aim of destroying the danger-ous annihilating mother (ibid., p. 129).

Furthermore, in Eigen's (1986) elaboration on blankness and mind-lessness in psychosis, he stated that, 'In psychosis, crucial aspects of external and psychic reality can be blanked out or distorted, nulled or feverishly heightened (e.g., denial, disavowal, or hallucination). Reality, as a whole undergoes a radical malformation or transformation' (p. 104). Images of being killed, the soul being murdered, depletion and a sense of dread coupled with deadness is common in moments like these. Eigen writes that, 'the psyche may so deplete or collapse into itself that it approximates a "return" to an inorganic (insensate) state. Freud depicts this as a death wish, a dying out of investment' (ibid., p. 105). The images of death, electric shock, crater, nothing-empty, and hearing voices pushing or threatening to push her/him to death could also be a desire to return to an insensate state, a state where there is no excess and something goes blank. Bion (1967) postulated that in moments like these the patient still retains a contact with reality, but it is 'masked by the dominance, in the patient's mind and behaviour, of an omnipotent phantasy that is intended to destroy either reality or awareness of it, and this to achieve a state that is neither life, nor death' (p. 64). What is the space for the inorganic and the inanimate in our psychic reality? Can it be understood beyond aggression as a quest for rest? What does the quest for rest tell us about a desire to end one's life, distinct from the desire to sleep, but a desire for an end?

These questions around the suicidal subject have been closely related to reflections on the nature and structure of the psyche. This has taken me to texts and thinkers that could allow me to further understand the distinctions between the psychotic and the melancholic as well as the point of convergence between the same. Given the prevalent discourse represented in the Mental Health Care Bill[4], I found it important to think about what kind of subject positions are made available in the moment of suicide, in an attempt to understand the complexity of this subject position and its interplay with the socio-political and the psychological. While working with subjects in the clinic, I found myself thinking about the meta-psychological premises of what was being manifested and communicated while also attempting to keep a dialogue going with historical context. What are the symptoms created by the culture of the university, as seen in the university clinic? If the university is functioning as ego ideal, in what ways are the subjects of the university space negotiating their ties to the community? What kind of fantasy does a university with a clinic create? And further, can ideology and empathy exist together? If one is to attempt to understand what the subject desires from the university, it would also become important to think about what the university is beginning to signify for the subject.

---

[4] As stated before, the bill proposes a largely biomedical model of diagnosis and care that does not repeal Section 309 but specifically adds the presumption of 'mental illness' (unless proved otherwise) as a determinant of the event.

A Return to Freud

Yet there remains a difficulty in locating the question of suicide (as an act) within the given setting (of the university and the clinic in the university), since the act marks the setting through different signifiers, but does not necessarily represent itself constantly. This remains a difficulty encountered by this work in thought and in writing. In an attempt to address this question, I found it useful to shift from the question of what is suicide or how it came to be constructed thus, to where one can locate that which is prior to the act of suicide—a propensity, or a tendency towards it.

Where[5] does one begin to understand the question of suicide: the question it poses in its attempt, and the questions it leaves in its wake. How would one define suicide, or how would we *know* suicide, since any elaboration of that would always be post-mortem, bringing with itself its inherent unknowability, similar to the one brought on with death. From the onset itself then, suicide possesses us with the problem of representation, the problem where something is over-represented, in theory and understanding, but remains inherently unpresentable.[6] Because we can never truly *know* suicide. This work then does not claim to know suicide but attempts to engage with that which is *suicidal*, presenting itself in moments, acts, and states. It further asks, who is the subject of suicidality, what is this subject position and furthermore, how to engage with what it is communicating. The exploration of suicidality, then, is not just limited to what one hears in the clinic in explorations of suicidal thoughts but also in moments of protest, where institutional violence is dubbed as institutional murder. Suicide is defined as the 'action of killing oneself' while suicidality is defined as 'the tendency to commit suicide'. It is this tendency, before the action, that I wish to explore further.

Perhaps an exploration of suicidality will also open up the question of what is finally termed suicide. Suicide as not just a self-explanatory

---

[5] The question of where, as opposed to the question of how – for me this marks the shift towards the understanding around 'drive'

[6] Mitra, W. (2017) Personal communication

term implying the killing of one's self with the finality attached to it, but recovering from this finality the interplay between the pleasure principle and the death drive, which remains a tightrope walk throughout life. In an attempt to understand the relationship between the two, one must begin with Freud, for he does not rely on an anatomical notion of life and death. The drive to death, as he understands it, is not the limit point of life but as something present from the beginning, thus constituting the entire psychic apparatus as an attempt to defend against a familiar known.

Freud (1919) defined the uncanny as 'that species of the frightening that goes back to what was once well known and had long been familiar' (p.124). In contrast, Jentsch, in his understanding of the uncanny, took the concept back to a sense of intellectual uncertainty where that which is novel and unknown produces such a feeling. Freud, on the other hand, returned to language in an attempt to trace how something familiar can also become frightening.

Using Hoffman's tale of the Sandman, Freud moves one towards the importance of the idea of the double. The Sandman represents an uncanny figure that takes on different forms in the protagonist Nathaniel's life from a childhood tale, to a figure that follows one around, eventually knowing full well that Nathaniel would jump from the bell tower. But how did the Sandman know? The double initially represented the 'insurance against the extinction of the self' (1919, p. 142) stemming from a sense of primary narcissism, but when this stage of narcissism is surmounted, the qualities of the double reverse themselves into becoming 'the uncanny harbinger of death' (ibid.). As the double developed newer meanings in later stages of ego development, Freud links it to the critical agency of the ego (also known as the ego Ideal).

Though the relationship between this critical agency and the rest of the ego is elaborated, it however does not explain the feeling of the uncanny. Freud went on to link the feeling of uncanniness to *unintended repetition* (ibid., p. 144) which, in his hypothesis, comes from an unconscious compulsion to repeat, and it is this 'inner compulsion to repeat (that) is perceived as uncanny' (ibid., p. 145). This compulsion to repeat remains powerful as it finds its roots in the 'old animistic view of the universe' (ibid., p. 147) which leaves traces in the psyche, even though it remains a stage that one has passed through. Freud stated that, 'the uncanny element is actually nothing new or strange, but something that was long familiar to the psyche and was estranged from it only through being repressed' (ibid., p. 148).

In *Beyond the Pleasure Principle*, Freud (1920) defined the pleasure principle as 'a strong tendency within the psyche, but is opposed by certain other factors or circumstances' (p. 47). He elaborated these factors to be the sources of unpleasure which come from a conflict with(in) the psychic apparatus through the process of development, along with a sense of perceptual unpleasure from without, which is recognized as danger. In response to this danger, one can have Fear, an inner state which remains anticipatory even though the nature of danger is not known, a sense of Dread—where there is a specific object of danger identified, or Fright—which possesses an element of surprise. He emphasized the difference between these, as he is struck by the fact that despite these responses, one might repeat a certain behaviour or situation though it has been a source of unpleasure, as if beyond the dominion of the pleasure principle 'where unpleasure leads ultimately to the gain of pleasure' (ibid., p. 55). He described this tendency as more primal and quite independent of the pleasure principle. This compulsion to repeat comes in the service of memory, where, that which is not remembered is repeated and this repetition is not (just) situated between the conscious and the unconscious of the psychic apparatus, but between the ego and that which is repressed. What complicates this compulsion further is the fact that most of the ego remains unconscious as well, and the nature of this excitation is not just external but also internal. He thus described the drives as 'the most abundant source of such excitation ... which represent all those manifestations of energy that originate in the inner depths of the body and are transmitted to the psychic apparatus' (ibid., p. 74).

Freud located this compulsion to repeat in the play of children and in the manifestation of transference. His contention seems to be that each repetition seeks to convert that which is passive into that which is active and in doing so, adds to a sense of control and command. It is this 'replication of the original experience' (ibid., p. 76) that becomes a source of pleasure as opposed to the novelty of a new experience. In describing the relationship between drives and the compulsion to repeat, Freud surmised a *universal attribute* (ibid.) not just of the drives themselves, but all organic life: 'a powerful tendency inherent in every living organism to restore a prior state' (ibid.). One can wonder then, what is the nature of this prior state? Where does the compulsion to repeat find its allegiance now that we know its spaces of outlet?

In the attempt to answer that, what is uncanny and beyond the pleasure principle, begin to dialogue. Freud postulated that 'the goal of all life is death' (ibid., p. 78). He seems to be talking about a period in the evolution of the organism where the inevitability of death was more pronounced, when the idea of natural death had not yet appeared, and the species had not evolved enough to extend life. As the species progressed, however, the course of life has increased and the detours to achieve death have become more complex. He further stated that 'the organism wants only to die in its own particular way' (ibid., p. 79) and yet the preservatory drives appear to be working in the opposite direction. Freud himself appeared to be disturbed by this postulation and it seems unimportant to prove whether these drives exist or not, but instead think about what this turn to the death drive allowed him to understand about the human psyche. Coming from the context of the war and violence he was enmeshed in, this turn might have been useful in attempting to understand something about the civilization at that point as well. The world today seems to be at a similar cross point where violence and war have taken on a different form; can the notion of the death drive then open up the question of the rise in suicides and what it is communicative of? One cannot deny that we are embedded at this point in a culture that is warring with what it could stand for and what it would like to stand for. Freud seems to be alerting us to the fact that there remains a tension, an interplay between the two, and in the moments when it presents itself, there would be a complex interplay of the drive, the object it chooses, the compulsion to repeat within the matrix of transference. A further question becomes, what is the death drive's relationship to the object, and what kind of object does it choose?

In my reading, the tension between the death drive and the tendency to suicide seem to remain undercurrents in Freud's later writing, though interestingly, he never dedicates a paper to it. The theme presents itself in his case histories as well; in Dora's dream through the note she writes, in Schreber's memoir in his own attempts and his brother's (and possibly father's) acts of suicide, and in Wolfman through his sister's suicide. In attempting to understand the death drive and its relationship to the object, one possible route could be exploring the idea of melancholia as Freud has set up.

Suicidality and Melancholia

Melancholia takes on many different forms, which are difficult to club together and need to be differentiated from the 'normal affect of mourning' (Freud 1917, p. 203). Both, mourning and melancholia, have similar causes as far as environmental conditions are concerned and are represented in both psychogenic and somatic manifestations. It is a response to a loss of a loved one or an abstraction of some kind, where melancholia would be a pathological disposition of the process of mourning. Temporality and duration in this case separating the pathological from the normative, and for a brief moment, Freud also wonders why mourning in itself is not referred for treatment. The role of the social comes in as a crucial interlude which will decide what needs treatment and what will pass. From the onset, one is governed by something also external to oneself, which impacts and decides the healthy temporality and duration of dealing with loss.

What further separates melancholia from mourning is the *disorder of self-esteem* (ibid., p. 204) which ends up 'intensifying into a delusionary expectation of punishment' (ibid.). Enthralled by what is lost, the melancholic cannot stop thinking about loss and will not move quickly towards replacing the lost object with a new love object. The characterization of the economies of pain might allow one to get a sense of why the psyche indulges in this degree of unpleasure. It is difficult to give up an already established libidinal investment even when another substitute is present such that there is a turning away from reality towards the lost object in an attempt for hallucinatory wish fulfilment. Is it this turning away from reality that takes melancholia close to psychosis? Is that the hallmark of psychosis? How would one differentiate it from love? It is only through the work of mourning where hyper-cathected libidinal energy is brought up and detachment of the libido takes place, that the ego can eventually be uninhibited and free once again. What makes mourning different from melancholia, is also that in melancholia 'the object may not really have died, but may instead have been lost as a love-object' (ibid., p. 205). It may not even be clear, consciously, that someone has been lost, and even if the *whom* is clear, there can still be a lack of awareness on *what* has been lost. In both cases, there is an inhibition of the ego caused by the loss, but in the case of melancholia it is difficult to see what the person is so absorbed with, as this is a 'loss of an object that is withdrawn from consciousness' (ibid.).

The melancholic perceives the ego to be empty and assumes it to be 'worthless, incapable of functioning and morally reprehensible, he is filled with self-reproach, he levels insults against himself and expects ostracism and punishment' (ibid., p. 206). This eventually results in an 'overcoming of the drive which compels everything that lives to cling to life' (ibid.). However, in doing so, the melancholic may not be far from the truth and may actually be close to a keener sense of his self. There seems to be a lack of shame however, almost as if 'insistent talkativeness, (is) taking satisfaction from self-exposure' (ibid., p. 207). Thus giving a correct description of his psychological situation: communicating what has been lost to the ego. In melancholia 'one part of the ego presents itself to the other, critically assesses it and, so to speak, takes it as its object' (ibid., p. 207). What do we know of this critical agency that at this point becomes split off from the ego? Who does it owe its allegiances to—the forces of Eros or the drive to Death? Instead of withdrawal of libido from the love object and a displacement onto another one, the libido is withdrawn into the ego such that the ego forms an identification with the abandoned love object. 'The shadow of the object fell upon the ego, which could now be condemned by a particular agency as an object, as the abandoned object' (ibid., p. 209). One can wonder then what the role of the Super ego is, in this moment when this conflict between object loss and ego loss is lodged in the space between the critical agency of the ego and the ego itself. A contradictory stance appears here, where a 'strong fixation on the love object must be present and on the other there must be minimal resistance in the form of object investment' (ibid.). Freud used Otto Rank here to arrive at the conclusion that the object choice 'occurred on a narcissistic foundation' (ibid.). In such a case, the conflict with the love object does not result in the giving up of the love relation. What in this moment remains in the unconscious? The conflict? The narcissistic investment? Or the contradictory nature of retaining one while giving up the other, making it difficult to separate the 'what' from the 'whom' in the nature of loss? Though identification is an ambivalent way of picking out the object, here the ego wants to *assimilate the object* (ibid., p. 209). As such, a narcissistic type of object choice could be a (pre)disposition to melancholia.

In narcissistic identifications, object cathexis is abandoned while in hysterical identification it persists and manifests through different means: possibly the use of the body. Furthermore, Freud located melancholia between mourning, narcissistic object choice and narcissism. He further went on to differentiate obsessional neurosis from melancholia. In the former, a state of depression can be reached without a drawing in of the libido into the ego. In melancholia, there is a conflict due to ambivalence. He stated, 'if the love of the object, which cannot be abandoned, has fled into narcissistic identification, hatred goes to work on this substitute object, insulting it, humiliating it, making it suffer and deriving a sadistic satisfaction from that suffering' (ibid., p. 211). The attempt in both illnesses is to torment the loved one without having to express this openly. The erotic cathexis (love investment) has 'undergone a second fate: in part it has regressed to identification, but it has also been moved back, under the influence of the conflict of ambivalence, to a sadistic stage to which it is closer' (ibid., p. 211).

Here Freud (1917) links the tendency (inclination) to suicide with this stage of sadism. He states, the ego can only kill itself when it is able to treat itself as an object because of the return of object investment, if it is able to direct hostility that applies to the object back against itself and represents the original reaction of the ego against objects in the outside world (ibid., p. 212).

The ego returns to a primal state surrounded by a vast narcissistic libido, regressing to a narcissistic object choice, thus making the object itself more powerful than the ego even though the object has been given up.

Thus, it seems, in the Freudian understanding, the notion of the death drive, its relationship to the pleasure principle, the compulsion to repeat and its uncanny relationship to the inorganic become focal points in understanding suicidality. Sadism, masochism and narcissism also become important points of further exploration. For the clinician, then, the concept of melancholia offers a route to explore the nature of suicidal thoughts (and there must be other routes of exploration as well.) Setting up the metapsychology at this point becomes important to further elaborate what one sees in the clinic, as it is work in the clinic itself that has informed these research questions to begin with. Possibly the notion of the death drive can further elaborate where the tendency to suicide is located, not just in the reasons for referral, but also beyond it. Is there something about suicidality that remains present in all of us?

The Concept of the Death Drive

To understand the notion of the death drive, one would have to return to what Freud meant by his conception of drives. The understanding of the drives forms the base of the economic model in Freud. This model is one of the premises for his concept of the unconscious. In *Drives and Their Fates* (1915)[7] he defines drive as 'the real motive force behind the advances that have brought the nervous system, with

---

[7] Initially translated as 'Instincts and their Vicissitudes' (1915) in the Standard Edition.

its infinite capabilities, to its present height of development' (p. 16). The difficulty with taking into account the notion of the death drive or the drive in general ties closely with the notion of the unconscious, which with its conception makes man a different kind of subject, a subject who is no longer in conscious control. Freud further stated that 'drive emerges as a concept on the borderline between the mental and the physical—the psychic representation of stimuli flowing into the psyche from inside the body, or the degree of work-load imposed on the psyche as a result of its relation to the body' (ibid., p.16).

The aim of the drive is satisfaction while satisfaction as a phenomenon in itself is premised on the pleasure principle, which attempts to avoid unpleasure and gain pleasure. He defined the pleasure principle as 'a strong tendency within the psyche, but is opposed by certain other forces or circumstances, so that the final outcome cannot possibly always accord with the said tendency is favor of pleasure' (Freud 1920, p. 47). But the psyche constantly attempts to is also always in an attempt to maintain stability. The reality principle inhibits the pleasure principle in service of the self-preservation drives of the ego whose ultimate aim remains pleasure but will be willing to tolerate a degree of unpleasure in order to get there. The pleasure principle ties more closely to the sexual drives, such that they can gain hold of the entire psychic apparatus in service of pleasure. The displacement by the reality principle of the pleasure principle does account for some instances of unpleasure, but not the more intense ones.

During the process of the development of the ego, the division and conflict of the drives, which are different at different stages of ego development become another source of unpleasure. The energy in the psychic apparatus is derived from innate drive impulses, but not all these impulses are given access to the same phase of development. Freud postulates that there are 'numerous occasions where individual drives, or elements of individual drives, prove to be incompatible in their aims and demands with all those others that are capable of joining together to yield the all-embracing unity of the ego' (ibid., p. 48).

The ego in its formation and development is the first to perceive the drives and eventually attempt to control them. The id impulses, which are akin to drive impulses, exert a degree of unpleasure upon the ego in the process of its development. Freud elaborated that the 'ego very largely develops out of identifications which take place of cathexes generated by the id and then abandoned, and that the first of such identifications routinely assume the role of a special judgement entity within the ego, and set about countering the ego' (Freud 1923, p. 138). The formulation of the Super ego or ego Ideal appears to be a perception of, and an attempt to control, drive impulses. This part of the psyche comes into being through the resolution of the Oedipus Complex, which represents the first identifications in the psyche. In the process of sublimating the object cathexis of the Oedipus Complex, a de-mergence of drives takes place, such that the libido directed towards the object (in this case the mother and father) is desexualized and directed back into the ego. This de-mergence also results in the release of destructive components which cannot be annexed by the ego. Freud anticipated that the ego 'through the work it does to bring about identification and sublimations it helps the death drive to assert control over the libido, but it thereby runs the risk of itself becoming the object of the death drives and thus perishing' (ibid., p. 146).

The role of the ego ideal becomes important here, especially in understanding the ego alterations around drive. According to Freud, 'our social feelings rest on identification with other people on the basis of the same ego ideal' (ibid., p. 127). Along with carrying a moral character and a relationship to the external, the ego ideal is also intimately tied to the Id as Freud cautioned us that 'early conflicts of the ego with the object cathexis of the id can be continued later on in conflicts with their successor the super ego' (ibid., p. 128). The relationship between the ego and the ego ideal are premised on what Freud called an unconscious guilt feeling, as though the ego resists getting better and, on the contrary, denies any attempt of the same. This is what he termed the negative therapeutic reaction where it is the 'Guilt feeling that finds gratification in illness' (ibid., p. 140). Similar feelings of inferiority and guilt are seen in obsessional neurosis and in melancholia. In the first case, the guilt feeling is extreme but the ego does not feel it to be justified. It rejects the feeling completely, since they are about impulses outside the ego, the feeling itself is unconscious to the ego and the Super ego has closer ties to the Id. In melancholia, however, the object being critically received has been established within the ego through the process of identification such that

> the destructive component has lodged itself in the super ego and then turned against the ego. What thereupon prevails in the super ego is not unlike a pure form of the death drive, indeed it quite often succeeds in driving the ego to its death if the ego doesn't manage to keep its oppressor at bay by switching off (ibid., p. 143).

This is the only circumstance in which Freud conceives of the Ego's capacity to drive itself to death. In melancholia, the ego feels persecuted by the super ego instead of feeling loved as 'confronted by the massive danger in the objective world that it believes itself powerless to overcome; it sees itself as deserted by all the forces that could have protect it, and lets itself die (ibid., p. 148).

I became curious about the nature of the relationship between the ego and the ego ideal at this juncture, such that death in itself becomes a possibility. Freud would indicate this relationship to be a masochistic one. In 'The Economic Problem of Masochism', Freud stated the precarious predicament of the psyche through its relationship to a tendency towards stability. It would appear in his understanding that the

> nirvana principle would be entirely in the service of the death (drive), whose aim is to conduct the restlessness of life into the stability of an inorganic state, and it would have the function of giving warnings against the life (drive)—the libido—which try to disturb the intended course of life (Freud 1942, p. 275).

Driven by a tendency towards stability, the drives originated from the transition of the inorganic to the organic, and are constantly in contact with each other such that their mergence and de-mergence will create different states within the psyche.

In understanding Sadism and Masochism, Freud defined masochism as a partial drive of sadism turning back into the ego. The ego that wants to be treated like a helpless naughty child, carries a sense of unconscious guilt which manifests as a need for punishment. In 'Beyond the Pleasure Principle' (1920) he stated 'Where the primal sadism element does not undergo any mitigation or dilution, the outcome is an erotic life marked by the familiar ambivalence of love and hate' (p. 94). Further, in the *Economic Problem of Masochism* (1942) he postulated, 'the death drive which is operative in the organism – primal sadism – is identical with masochism (p. 278). In the resolution of the oedipal complex, the destructive elements released into the ego appear to be the ones that wreak havoc. Since 'the super ego retained essential features of the introjected persons—their strength, their severity, their inclination to supervise and to punish' (ibid., p. 281) the ego's response to it, and masochism as a concept, become important in this light. He further postulated that

> moral masochism becomes a classical piece of evidence for the existence of fusion of instinct (merger of drive). Its danger lies in the fact that it originates from the death (drive) and corresponds to the part of that (drive) which has escaped being turned outwards as a drive of destruction. But since, on the other hand, it has the significance of an erotic component, even the subject's destruction of himself cannot take place without libidinal satisfaction (ibid., p. 283).

From these papers it appears that the drives play an important role both in the formation of the ego and the ego Ideal such that a de-mergence and release of destructive energy and sublimation predicate the development of the same. For the purpose of the present study, the development of ego and the ego ideal would gain a significance that will be discussed subsequently. The complexity of Freud's understanding lies in the fact that the drive, the formation of the ego and the ego ideal, their relationship to the Id and subsequently the pathologies and conditions they create cannot be understood as a singularity in themselves. Their interplay becomes important in defining the very nature of the drives, which presents itself in the form of the psychic polarities of active/passive (biology), ego and outside world (real) and pleasure/unpleasure (economic). And so, the drives are, to a certain extent, always predicated on a degree of ambivalence, in their aim and their representation making them impossible to study in their pure form.

To understand the drive, one would have to look at the derivatives of the drive and their role in the formation of the structure of the psyche. The theory of the drives in itself has occupied a contested space in the history of psychoanalysis. It marks a clear split in post-Freudian work between those who consider it conceptually significant and those who do not. In the process of putting together this chapter, I was guided by a sense of lag and gap that I experienced while working in the clinic. The subjects I worked with and their preoccupations with death often made me wonder about the nature of our technique. At moments I would find it difficult to refute their preoccupations and the scheme of logic their thoughts followed, and yet there remained a clear awareness that one must remain life-avowing. I found it difficult to stay close to that, without understanding what this preoccupation with death meant, not just in the subjects I worked with, but in the psyche itself.

Post-Freudian Understanding of the Death Drive

In the process of the review, I found it important to depart from the standard edition translation of Freud's work to the Penguin edition translations, which are more recent. This, in my understanding, is an important theoretical difference. The initial translation of the term *'Trieb'* has been considered problematic by a host of psychoanalytic thinkers and translators. The term was formerly translated to 'instinct,' by James Strachey in the Standard Edition of Freud's work. Critics have argued that this translation alters the import of the term *'Trieb'* on Freud's metapsychology, reducing it to a biological determinant. These re-translators request a 'degree of terminological latitude, and suggest that when *Trieb* is used to mean a goal seeking force, a vector...it is best translated as *drive'*. (Whiteside, 2005, p.xxxiii) To review further how drive has been understood conceptually post Freud, I read thinkers who had marked this difference in their theoretical interludes. I noticed most of these thinkers were French, and there was an emphasis on language and translation being brought to light in the introduction of their works. The role of language in understanding the psyche thus gained significance in my mind and this work draws from French psychoanalysts who seemed preoccupied with the same.

Jacques Lacan (1964) built upon Freud's understanding of the drive and contended that the Drive is a fundamental concept of psycho-analysis, along with the unconscious, repetition and transference. In returning to the concept of the Drive, he followed Freud's seminal paper 'Drive and Their Fates'.[8] In this paper, Freud demarcated four elements of the concept of the drive: pressure (thrust), aim, object and source. Using these four, Lacan predicated the question of the drive in the question of what becomes the Freudian Field. The aim of the drive is satisfaction, but satisfaction in itself remains an impossibility. Freud too indicated that the object of the drive is important in as much as it can satisfy its aim. Lacan, taking this postulation a step further, stated, 'the drive moves around the object, The drive tricks the object' (1964, p. 168). The relationship between drive and object can only be further illuminated by the path taken by a drive. Further, he stated, 'The whole point of the article is to show us that with regard to the biological finality of sexuality, namely, reproduction, the drives, as they present themselves in the process of psychical reality, are partial drives' (ibid., p.175).

To expand on this further, Lacan arrived at the polarities of psychic life as understood by Freud. These are between the ego and the outside world (real), pleasure and unpleasure (economic) and active/passive (biology). Through active and passive, Freud attempted to explore the drive fates of reversal into the opposite and turning onto oneself. Lacan understood this polarity as significant for grammatical reasons, in the way they constitute the subject. By understanding the movement in voyeurism, exhibitionism and sadomasochism, Lacan proposed that

[8] Initially translated as 'Instincts and their Vicissitudes' (1915) in the Standard Edition.

'what is fundamental at the level of each drive is the movement outwards and back in which it is structured' (1964, p. 177). The drive follows a circular path, and what is new with the drive is the appearance of the subject. In this understanding, the subject of the drive is a headless subject, such that 'it is only with its appearance at the level of the other that what there is of the function of the drive may be realized' (ibid., p.178). Thus, the drive predates the subject.

In Lacan, drive represents a stationary tension such that 'the tension is always loop-shaped and cannot be separated from its return to the erogenous zone' (ibid., p.179). The erogenous zone is also its source, with a complex location between the inside and the outside. Here, he also makes a distinction between satisfaction as aim and auto-eroticism indicating the nature of the object. The object of the drive is understood as 'the presence of a hollow, a void, which can be occupied, Freud tells us, by any object, and whose agency we know only in the form of the lost object, the petit a' (ibid., p.180). It is precisely this nature of the object that makes satisfaction both impossible and partial such that nothing will satisfy the drive 'except by circumventing the eternally lacking object' (ibid.). Further he indicated that the drive does not follow a maturational process from one partial drive to another and is not created by an intervention from the field of the drive but 'by the inter-vention, the overthrow, of the demand of the Other' (ibid.). This dimension of the Other occupies an important position in Lacan's metapsychology.

The Cartesian subject, in Lacan's understanding is a Barred Subject, acquiring certainty at the level of enunciation, 'constituted as a secondary relationship to the signifier' (ibid., p. 141). It is in dif-ferentiating itself from the signifier that the subject comes into being and 'thus is marked the first split that makes the subject as such dis-tinguish himself from the sign in relation to which, at first he has been able to constitute himself as a subject (ibid.). In this understanding then, the ego comprises the subject's relation to the signifiers within both orders: of the imaginary and the symbolic. Furthermore, 'It is in the locus of the Other that he (the subject) begins to constitute that truthful lie by which is initiated that which participates in desire at the level of the unconscious' (ibid., p. 144). Here, one can see the complexity of inside and outside that Lacan constantly plays with, such that even the transference, in his understanding, would be enacted in the field of the Other. Thus, he postulated the unconscious as 'inside that subject, but which can be realized only outside, that is to say, in that locus of the Other in which alone it may assume its status' (ibid., p. 147). Here, the relationship between the imaginary and the symbolic both become important in the constitution of the subject who is also marked by the real, through which the unconscious would present itself.

According to Lacan, each partial drive has a partial object, which is delineated by a specific verb and finds its source in a particular erogenous zone. Thus, rejecting the hypothesis of only one drive, namely the genital drive. Further he stated, 'the course of the drive is the only form of transgression that is permitted to the subject in relation to the pleasure principle' (ibid., p. 183), as the drive is in search of *Jouissance*, which is beyond the pleasure principle. Jouissance, much like Lacan's other concepts, carries a connotation that is difficult to translate into English. Though it is often translated as pleasure, there is an intolerable excitation, a deadliness attributed to this degree of pleasure, as though the distinction of pleasure and unpleasure would collapse at the moment of Jouissance. Precisely this course of the drive presenting itself as a 'montage—having neither head nor tail' (ibid., p. 169) and its search makes every drive a death drive, circular and repetitive in its nature, attempting to go beyond the pleasure principle. Thus, Lacan restored drive as a fundamental concept in understanding repetition and transference in the field of the Other, taking it away from a biological understanding closer to a symbolic one, such that the networks of signifiers and the pulsation of the unconscious show us a continuous series of arrangements between what works out for the subject, and what does not.

Jean Laplanche (1970), in his work entitled *Life and Death in Psychoanalysis,* attempted to relook at Freud's understanding of the Death Drive by examining the problematics and contradictions inherent in his theorizations of sexuality, the ego, and the theory of drives. He did not intend to establish the existence of the drive or its location, but attempted to locate it historically in Freud's work, so as to establish an understanding around the concept of the drive and its significance for psychoanalysis as a praxis. Laplanche put forth two assumptions in the beginning of his argument which allude to the presence of the death drive:

> at least two intentions coincide in the affirmation of the death drive, as it appears Beyond the Pleasure Principle: to reaffirm the fundamental economic principle of psychoanalysis, and that in the most radical form: the tendency to zero; to give a metapsychological status, within the theory of drives, to the increasingly numerous and impressive discoveries of psychoanalytic inquiry concerning the register of 'aggressiveness' and destructiveness' (1970, p. 85).

In his reading of Freud, Laplanche noticed that there is an absence of a theoretical recognition of aggressiveness prior to Freud's 1920 paper 'Beyond the Pleasure Principle' and a failure to see the primacy of self-aggression. He clarified that Freud's preoccupations with these questions, however, predated this paper, citing an example in the 1915 essay 'Drive and Their Fates' where Freud attempted to understand love, hate, ambivalence and sadomasochism. In Laplanche's understanding, the affirmation of the death drive does not come from the fact that it now has a theory around it, but from the idea that 'aggressiveness is first of all directed against the subject and, as it were, stagnant within him, before being deflected towards the outside' (ibid., p. 86). *Primary Masochism* becomes a massive evidence which predicated Freud's 1920 thesis.

In understanding aggressiveness, Laplanche inserted the important distinction between non-sexual and sexual, further stating that the mergence demergence of drives (which he termed 'propping') is 'that leaning of the nascent sexuality on nonsexual activities, but the actual emergence of sexual activities is not yet there.' (ibid., p. 88). To avoid the confusion of the slippages in Freud's writing between that which is sexual and that which is non-sexual, Laplanche, in his writing, limited this to terminology of sadistic and masochistic to represent 'tendencies, activities, fantasies etc. that necessarily involve, either consciously or unconsciously, an element of sexual excitement or enjoyment' (ibid., p. 87). This does not imply that there is no non-sexual aggressiveness, nor does it negate the premise that sadism carries non-sexual influences. Further he stated, 'sexuality appears as a drive that can be isolated and observed only at the moment at which nonsexual activity, the vital function, becomes detached from its natural object or loses it' (ibid., p. 88). Further, Laplanche attempted to establish that 'we never have to deal with pure life-drives and death-drives at all, but only with combinations of them in different degrees' (ibid., p. 96).

Laplanche, in an attempt to understand the 'Economic Paradox of the Death Drive', revisited Freud's conception of Eros, repetition compulsion, the drives in themselves, and the people who influenced Freud's understanding of homeostasis and constancy, including Fechner, Breuer and Helmholtz. He reviewed the significance of the self-phase/reflexive phase, the priority of zero over constancy and the repetition compulsion. He also attempted to account for the difficulty in grasping the concept as it moves from a biologism, to psychophysiology, to a dualism. Coupled with a confusion around translation and a reduction of theory to just his psycho-biographical, Laplanche cautioned that a structural tie, in Freud's theory, might have been missed such that 'in neglecting to relate the compulsion of the death drive to everything that prefigures or prepares in in other configurations of Freud's work' (ibid., p. 112). Drawing from a Lacanian understanding of Jouissance, he concluded by stating 'the death drive is the very soul, the constitutive principle of libidinal circulation' (ibid., p. 124).

Andre Green (1999), in *The Work of the Negative*, attempted to provide a 'model of the intrapsychic consequences of severe aggression, which Andre Green subsumes under Freud's concept of the death drive' (Kernberg 1999, p. xii). By introducing the concept of the Negative, he relooks at psychic activities such as repression, denial, disavowal, negation and foreclosure in an attempt to understand their relationship to drives and what he terms as their *objectalizing* and *disobjectalizing* function. He reviewed Klien, Winnicott, Bion, Lacan along with Freud's metapsychology to expand on the notion of the death drive as an important concept to understand the work of the negative.

Green noted that there no longer remains a consensus among psychoanalysts on the concept of the drives, and particularly, of the death drive. Though, theoretically, a space has been given to aggressivity in post-Freudian psychoanalysis, along with a consensus on the notion of psychic conflict (though the ways of representation and the aims and sources may differ). He further stated, 'one of the arguments advanced most frequently by the adversaries of the death drive is to maintain that it is difficult to see how one can apply the characteristics described for the sexual drive to the death drive (source, pressure, aim, object.)' (1999, p. 83). He contended this understanding by pointing out what this assumption misses:–'fundamental drive conflict corresponds in Freud to an exigency, that is to say, of explaining the fact that conflict can be repeated, displaced, transposed and that its permanence resists all transformations of the psychical apparatus' (ibid.).

In an attempt to establish the importance of the death drive, Green began with two propositions: firstly, that one cannot talk about the death drive without talking about the life drives as they 'form an indissociable conceptual pair' (ibid., p. 84). Secondly, the drive is a given and it is there, but 'the object reveals the drives'. In other words, though it does not create it, the drive is brought into existence through the object. He further compared this to Winnicott's idea of *found created.* He marked the difference between the life drive and the death drive through objectalizing and deobjectalizing functions. According to Green, the life drive is capable of binding, unbinding and absorbing parts of the death drive. Its objectalizing function is defined as not just its relationship to form object relations, but also its capacity to transform 'structures into an object, even when the object is no longer directly involved' (ibid., p. 85). As long as there is a meaningful investment, the life drive can transform not just structures of the ego but psychic activity in such a way that 'it is the investment itself which is objectalised' (ibid., p. 85). This has important implications for the way we understand the play of drives and the formation of defence mechanisms. The death drive, on the other hand, can only unbind. It has a disobjectalizing function such that not just the object relations, but the ego itself can come under attack due to 'the fact itself of investment in so far as it has undergone the process of objectalisation' (ibid., p. 85).

Further, Green recognized the paradox of psychoanalytic experience in as much as 'the disobjectalising function, far from being confused with mourning, is the most extreme way of preventing the work of mourning which is at the centre of the transformation process characteristic of the objectalising function' (ibid., p. 86). Through this, he postulated the concept of 'negative narcissism' in an attempt to understand a movement towards zero level, whereas the deobjectalizing functioning focuses not on the objects or object relations, but the objectalizing function itself. Further, Green noted, 'the modes of action of drive (binding- unbinding) can be found in the ego, either because it carries the certificate of origin or because it mimes the drive functioning revealed by the object' (ibid., p. 87). Once more, the relationship between ego, object and drive gets highlighted as significant in understanding psychic conflict.

Through Green's emphasis on the work of the negative and relationship to the death drive, a link between the death drive and its representations in psychic conflict is highlighted. One can wonder then, what is the relationship of the death drive, at moments of interruption, in the process of mourning—in the work of the negative—and what it could possibly lend to an understanding of 'suicidality?'

From the above review it becomes important to note that defining suicide as an act remains a complex phenomenon with its inherent difficulties. The act in itself cannot be understood as purely psychological and requires an engagement with the socio-political factors at play, along with an understanding of the network of meaning that function at the level of culture in defining what would be termed a suicide.

Furthermore, drawing from a psychoanalytic understanding, the role of fantasy has been highlighted as significant, as well as a movement towards psychosis in the conception of the subject. A question remains as to whether there are other ways to understand a movement towards suicide, not limiting to a flight into fantasy. In an attempt to elaborate this further, through Freud's work, this review tries to elaborate on the relationship between the ego and the ego ideal to further think about what makes suicide a possibility in the psyche. Bringing it closer to the present context of the university setting and the rise of suicide rates within this setting, the review moved to understanding suicidality, the tendency towards suicide. Here, the relationship of the psyche with drives became important, as highlighted in Freud's work. With the return to Freud to understand the nature of drives, the review further delved into the work of Lacan, Laplanche and Green in an attempt to understand whether the concept of the death drive can aid us in understanding something about suicidality within the university context; how do we decipher suicidality as a symptom and preoccupation in the subjects that come into a university clinic? What is the nature of work, with this kind of a symptom? What does it tell us about the particular context in which this research is placed?

CHAPTER 2

How Do We Engage with Suicidality?

Researching in the Clinic: Towards a Methodology

There are multiple questions and preoccupations that have constantly emerged in the process of this research. Some of these have been lingering prior to the conception of the present work, while others have developed from interactions with the university, and the clinic, as spaces. The main question this research attempts to grapple with is: how do we engage with suicidality—its expressions and communications—in the setting of a clinic situated within the university, in a context where universities in themselves are a site of considerable socio-political turbulence?

The Evolving Question

As stated in the Prologue, engaging with suicide, as an event that is difficult to think about and symbolize, has gained significant prominence for me, through my own life history. This desire to engage with the phenomenon initially came upon me as a *need* to understand the untimely loss of a friend, and the impact this loss had on me. The question presented itself as: *why would someone take their life? what would prompt that kind of a decision?* I think, at an affective level, these were my attempts to mourn and symbolize the nature of this loss and its untimeliness. Though the work of mourning remains a continuous process, these questions no longer grip me as a need to solve the riddle of this 'why,' but turn me towards other curiosities which further shaped the direction of the present work. This work is thus impacted by these prior questions through my life historical, but does not remain governed by them, alone.

The present times, in which this work has been thought about, have been turbulent in many ways. Apart from a life stage development that has taken place, as I moved from my Masters in Psychosocial Clinical Studies to my MPhil training in Psychoanalytic Psychotherapy and further still, there have been changes, both structurally and phenomenologically, within two identities that I had begun to occupy: the student in a university setting and a therapist in training.

As mentioned earlier, for my student identity, Rohith Vemula's death by suicide remains an important event. This tragedy brought to the forefront a series of questions and debates about the education systems, and the rising rates of suicide in the university space.[1] However, what appeared most significant to me was how the student community began to mourn Rohith—not just as a student, but as a *Dalit* student. The bringing together of caste and suicide has been significant for student movements that have followed in the wake of the incident, and has impacted a larger discourse around the 'university' as well. I hadn't considered or thought about the link between caste and suicide, until Rohith's death by suicide. This unfortunate event, forced me to think about my own privileges and blind spots, owing particularly to this reality.

For my therapist in training identity, the introduction of the Mental Health Care Bill, and the subsequent decriminalization of suicide, was a significant moment. The bill doesn't repeal section 309 of the IPC, but amends it to include 'mental illness'. Though decriminalization is a step in the right direction, the definition of mental illness within the

---

[1] Some of this has been discussed in greater detail in the previous chapter.

bill provoked a lot of questions in my mind. *How would the bill and the law constitute the subject of suicide?* And equally importantly, *how would the practitioner work with him/her?* What was this definition in the service of, given that the populations that are showing an increasing rate of suicide are usually from marginalized sections—farmers, Muslims, Dalits, even students. In the current political regime of the country, there have also been trigger groups and dissenting groups, constantly in conflict with the government. Another question that arises then is, *what could decriminalization of suicide come to mean, in the present context? What are the network of meanings being attributed to this act?*

With these questions in mind, I began my training within the context of a clinic located within a university. There was much anxiety and trepidation in this phase, from being assigned referral forms, to establishing contact, to initial consultations, to the process of therapy. As I navigated these various stages, I cannot say the initial hesitation ever went away completely, but a sense of method began to develop, along with a sensibility which further informed my work thereafter. I began to realize that what was being presented to me wasn't as much about *the act* of taking one's life but *a preoccupation* with it. It was sometimes represented in the form itself as 'suicidal ideations' or 'suicidal thoughts,' while at other times it found no mention in the form. It would find representation in speech, in moments where the subject would say: *I just want this all to end, I wonder what would happen if I just banged my car into a tree, I need to get out of this, I am drowning,* or even in more straightforward terms, *I plan to take my life in March 2018, it has to be done by then, this has to end.*

On hearing these, though a sense of a potential acting out would come to mind, what I seemed to be seeing was more a preoccupation with suicide: a tendency toward suicide began highlighting itself, each influenced, shaped, marked by a life history in a shared historical context. From here, the research question transitioned into a dialectic between suicidality, a tendency and suicide, the act. What was this suicidality trying to communicate? What could it tell us about the location of the subject, not just in their life history but their context as well? It became important, in my understanding, to decipher and engage with this suicidality if there was to be a possibility of working with it. To understand suicide as well, engaging with suicidality could allow us to gather a semblance of the constitution of the act itself. In bringing this symptom to dialogue, giving it a space for representation, perhaps we would be able to reach an ethics of care, which could inform a model of prevention.

A tension remains in my mind, especially around terminology, that hasn't been resolved during the course of this work: *how do I address this individual who occupies their patienthood, in both conscious and unconscious ways, enters the clinic with an awareness of some level of distress and a desire to communicate the same, while also occupying a position, within his/her own unique context, which in itself remains an important factor?* In understanding the nature of the subject, Parker (2005, cited in 2015) states that the subject is 'contradictory, divided between consciousness and what is unconscious, trying to make sense of reality that is not always clearly represented to it, struggling to hold together competing explanations of the world' (2015, p. 4). To use the word 'subject' here then, is to highlight that there is more than just a patienthood at play with(in) the individuals whose cases have been represented in the present work. This patienthood, however, has been the first point of contact; it is where the work began.

In the clinic, though working with the 'here and now' between the dyad occupied a centrality, I also began to think about my own subject position and what it brought to the nature of this interaction. The field between me (as the therapist) and the subject of the clinic, was in interaction with me (as a student) within the university as a space, a space which also had within it, this clinic. A space that was located within the context of considerable turmoil. This work then, attempts to reflect on these therapeutic encounters, within this context, while examining my own role, and movements among these various locations. Having terminated work in the clinic and in the process of reflecting on it, and going back to it, in both thought and writing, my sense was that I was looking at something more than patienthood and clinical presentation, where the term 'subject' appears to be more fitting to the representations being brought forth in this work. The subject, then is 'an agent of action combining awareness and forgetfulness, mindfulness and recklessness, reasoning and unacknowledged motives' (Branney 2008, p. 4).

The interplay between the subject and the environment is thus highlighted, which has also been methodologically important to the present work, not just because of the nature of the subject, but also to understand the complexity of suicidality in its manifestation and signification. My own subject position too, remains marked not just by the position of being a student, a trainee within the university clinic, along with my own life history and responses to the turbulence within these spaces, but also by P's loss, whose death by suicide becomes an event that I continue to process, as I am writing.

Setting up the Setting

The clinic has occupied a centrality in my experience of the university, owing to my choice of training. It is, however, located at the back corner of the university. Though it remains fairly accessible from the university main gate, a short walk away, it remains distant from the main administration offices and the classrooms where the undergraduate and postgraduate classes happen. By the location itself, there is an attempt to allow a certain degree of privacy for those who walk in and out of the clinic. There are five rooms, one after the other, connected by a corridor. From one side of the entrance, one is greeted by a dense green foliage, covered by a green sun roof. In case it rains, you can still walk through this corridor; but in the heat, sitting or standing there can be a sweltering experience. The walls are decorated with some forms of mud art, courtesy the design students. They fit in, without being too jarring. On the other side of the clinic, is a long corridor that connects it from the side of the classrooms. This corridor used to be empty, since no one would really venture to this side of the university, except for the design students whose studios are situated in this part of the university. On either side there are doors that break the continuity of the corridor from one side to the other, demarcating clearly the space of the clinic. The rooms are of different sizes and follow a descending order. The room one works in depends, to an extent, on who the subject is—whether adult or child—and to a great extent also on availability and the timing that suits both the subject and the therapist. I knew rather early on in my work that I preferred working in Clinic 4. It was relatively spacious and well-lit which I found quite facilitative.

Gradually, over the years, this corridor has come to be used more. From there being one or two students sitting around with a book or chatting here, it now sees groups of people, amid discussion, sometimes eating, sometimes singing. These conversations look captivating, and carry a certain intensity of sound and cackle. I, myself, have sat long hours in these corridors, waiting between sessions, sometimes reading, sometimes in conversation about the pedagogy of psychoanalysis. This corridor also now houses a makeshift canteen, and a musical jam room. The walls are covered with graffiti, some thought-provoking images and some downright outrageous, but both expressions and symbolizations of internal landscapes. There have been times when I have had to interrupt my appointment mid-session to shut the corridor door in order to reduce the sound factor. There have also been times when I have seen a breakdown in the corridor that doesn't cross the door and make it into the clinic. When the corridor is used, I've seen some curiously look in, or knock and ask what is going on, while some walk on, undisturbed by what might be going on behind these doors. A diligent guard bhaiya sits on one side, sometimes helping students fill forms, sometimes requesting them to quiet down. He always looks officious when he hands over forms to anyone from the team and very alarmed if he has some forms piled up. I've seen him sit and talk to the students when immediate help wasn't available; he could even give you a sense of what was bothering the student because he was the first contact.

The clinic rooms have been witness to multiple stories, different life histories, struggles and triumphs, crisis and breakthrough. Moments of silence and moments of enunciation, leaving both the subject and the therapist affected by the flow of communication, and the gaps and pauses in the same. The corridor outside, however, has seen something different: a kind of activity that doesn't enter the clinic but displays itself right outside it. Like spray cans and provocative images, loud death metal and drumming, sometimes a lone voice singing loudly to herself. Group discussions following general body meetings, over cigarette after cigarette. Conversations about the state and politics, or the nature of classroom discourse. And many a times, a friend, or a couple of friends, comforting someone in an inconsolable state. Of course, there might be other parts of the university where students sit around or draw on the walls, but this corridor always had an intriguing air to it. *With this clinic at the margins of the university, what was on display in the margins of this clinic?* I often wondered whether some sort of permissibility was granted to whatever was expressed in this corridor because of being located so close to the clinic, a clinic that stood for psychological well-being, while also acting in the service of individual feelings and realizations; never away from the community one came from, with the hope to maintain ties, with the endeavour to make care accessible, keeping in mind the multiple locations one was grappling with.

The number of people accessing the clinic has gradually been increasing. While those who come to the clinic are not only from the university, I would often wonder what kind of a space the clinic and its margins were becoming for students of the university. *What are the other avenues of psychological care available to the student community, especially those who do not come to the clinic?* The initial conception of this work might even have attempted to explore, through interviews and conversations, the nature of this care outside the clinic, in communities and student groups. That direction remains unexplored due to the lack of time. What takes on precedence, however, is the working of/in the clinic, which situates itself within the university as a space, with emphasis on the concept of suicidality.

Between the Questions and the Setting: Locating The 'I'

My research preoccupations followed my clinical work. Gradually, my interaction with subjects of the clinic raised questions that would follow me to classroom discussions and seminars. At moments, I would feel a chasm between what was being taught in the classroom and what was being brought to the clinic. Though the nature of what was taught remained complex, it lacked a context for where I was situated (in the process of being trained) and the subject positions of the people I worked with. As a result, metapsychology became important to me. Being exposed to thinkers who were far more advanced and could articulate, with both clarity and empathy, what their clinical experiences were, highlighted for me a requirement to go back to the basics; to attempt to bridge the gap between what I was being taught and what I was seeing. My sense was that if I could understand the larger metapsychological premises in a thinker's writing, I would be able to grasp more fully the techniques in question. What aided thinking around clinical work was supervision and self-work. While supervision opened up ways to think through cases, self-work allowed me to delve deeper into moments of being stuck as well as of trepidation. Though I was exposed to many states through the process of my clinical work, working with suicidal patients often took precedence, owing to my interest in formulating a research around it and the process of case assignment. I have often wondered how much my research interest impacted my work with the subject in both useful and not so useful ways. Whether the clinic can be a field for this kind of research work, or if another field should be sought out. Though the option of another field was left open in this work, I finally chose to use the work from the clinic. There was a clear desire in me to think further about the particularity of a university clinic.

It is in the process of working in the clinic that the research question gained sharper focus, shifting its object of enquiry to a dialectic between the act of suicide and the tendency towards it, i.e., suicidality. This clarity emerged with the culmination of my clinical work and in the writing of it. Though a movement towards tendency had taken place in the process of the work itself, in moments of enactment and transference with the subjects, a sharper question emerged during the writing of the clinical portfolio. The cases represented within this work are a product of ongoing processing and retrospective meaning making of work that has happened. While writing my portfolio, I was in the process of terminating work in the clinic. This termination allowed for a different kind of processing.

I have wondered about this act of looking back at these lived moments. Something feels so collected and thought through, in looking back. And yet, looking back, one sees how slowly things unfold; how patterns crystalize into semi-stable structures. How slowly they opened up, and yet how obvious some of them seem now. An obviousness only looking back can allow.

I wonder what gets lost when we are overcome by the present moment. Perhaps that is necessary too; a particular moment demands a specificity: of response, of affect, and of engagement. We unconsciously chose, assuming it's the best response to a moment. And yet, there are errors. But aren't we always attempting to make the best of a bad job? Unavoidably so, we give, we attempt to be what's needed in that moment. A confidant, a sounding board, a fresh set of eyes. Day after day, session after session, *we witness*. Another life unfolds, in all its ups and down. This isn't simple watching, or spectating. To bear witness is to move away from that which protects one from what is being seen. The witness becomes the memory of that which has changed. A memory that cannot be easily forgotten because it has a corporeal form. It is deposited within the body. In the eyes, the skin, the fingertips. It lingers in the *setting*.

But what defines the setting? Physically, the four walls protected by a door that reads *vacant* or *in session*. Pale yellow walls, with cracks and little marks of other inhabitants, which refuse to be erased. Sometimes a mouse trap, usually vacant. With a chair demarcated for one to witness, with a few other chairs and maybe a sofa. A couple of options. A wall hanging or a painting that sometimes catches the eye. A clock, keeping time, defining the session, in time. 50 minutes, give or take. Five or ten when things don't open or moments can't close. And yet despite its specificity, it feels continuous. Week after week, month after month, year after year.

The setting I was in, the setting that I also created, always had a notebook on the side. Just there, on the desk to my right, sometimes my left, if the room was different. A notebook and a pen. I wouldn't use it, except in the first few meetings, but it remained a part of the setting, even when I didn't. I would return to it after each session, and by a force of habit jot down a few things: the date, the day, the time, a signifier of the person whom I had met, and a few words to help me return to what we had talked about, what I had felt, what had seemed important in the moment.

I've wondered who this writing was for? A record of what has transpired? A way to contain my anxiety of being in the room? A proof of what has transpired? No... these seem distant from my experience of writing. At moments, in listening, more often than not, I feel written upon. Because to write, there needs to be contact, between pen and paper, and a necessary friction for the words to come out. That comes closest to my experience of the setting. The experience of sitting on that chair. This writing, for me, is reconnecting. Recording. Re-chording. Possibly also creating a dialogue between multiple impacts and responses. Creating, very slowly, a sense of response-ability, not devoid of its own stutters and stumblings of course, but a little surer of itself, for now.

It is a collection of these records, thoughts, interactions, this writing and a returning to it, that formed the case representations presented in this work. These narratives remain close to the experience of working with the subject; however, they are not the complete or the only representation of the subject or the work that was done. They are a representation of an engagement with a particular question: *how do we understand suicidality—its expressions and communications, in the setting of a clinic situated within the university, in a context where universities themselves are a site of considerable socio-political turbulence.* The work thus grapples with two settings—between the subject and the therapist in the clinic and the setting of the clinic within the university space.

The Psychoanalytic Tool Box

Before delving into the representations of chosen cases, it is important to foreground some psychoanalytic concepts that gained salience in the work with these subjects. Furthermore, this section also attempts to address whether a representation of larger socio-political forces can be deciphered in the process of clinical engagement with the subject. What kind of methodology would inform this kind of work, and what is its significance to the present study?

The Importance of Listening

My work in the clinic has been a part of a training programme in psychoanalytic psychotherapy. The nature of the work, therefore, from the outset, implies the presence of unconscious forces at play in the presentation of a symptom, in the modes of communication, in affect and thought, and in the dynamic relationship established with the subject, within the setting of the clinic. It is important to state here, that the work with these subjects began not with the intent to engage with the research question, but to process and work through the distress that was being brought to the clinic by the subject, through the *analytic association* forged between the subject and the therapist.

Psychoanalysis, as I have come to understand it, over the course of my training, is not just a method of diagnosis and treatment, but also a form of praxis, providing a model of being and constituting a subject in the 'here and now'. What became important for me, in working with these subjects, was the gap between what was said and what remained unsaid: the slips and pauses, the imagery that would come to mind while listening; and the impacts these communications would make once the clinical hour had passed. To listen psychoanalytically, as I understand it, requires me to attend to language and affect, not just in that which was said, but also in that which couldn't find words. Parallel to this, was an attempt to return to the history of the subject, his/her coming into being; and the impacts, conflicts, and resolutions, experienced in the constitution of the same. Theoretically, there remains sharp distinctions between what constitute the fundamental concepts of psychoanalysis and the nature of technique, and I struggled with what to attend to. What remained helpful in these moments was a healthy *scepticism* with a *free-floating attention,* being *reliably present* to the states brought in by the subject. It became important to me to provide a space to the subject to come into being, knowing in those moments that I had absolutely no idea what could emerge and the directions it could take. Befriending this *not knowing* has been the hardest task and yet the most vital ally to this work.

As I remain engaged in the process of developing my psychoanalytical sensibilities, I have come to an understanding that psychoanalysis is an engagement with the art of listening, communicating, and relating, with disciplined subjectivity. It offers

> a place to talk about life, explore one's truth, to taste experience, and perhaps build a capacity to let experience build. It recognizes, at least, like the poet, that creating language for the impact of events is never ending, that we hunger for language responsive to impact, a language for impact and response (Eigen 2005, p. 5).

It is this dialogue, between impact and response, that formed the crux of my work with subjects in the clinic. This dialogue that is constantly evolving a way of being. Always in the process of becoming, with each engagement with the other.

Transference and Countertransference

In an attempt to understand the relationship between the self and the other, the subject and the therapist, transference and countertransference become important tools for the therapist and the researcher. In the *Studies on Hysteria* (1895a) Freud referred to transference as a *false connection* that the patient wishes to establish with the person of the treating physician. In Dora's case (1905e), he stated that transferences are 'new editions or facsimiles of the impulses and fantasies which replace the earlier person by the person of the physician.' His pioneering work in this field, however, came across in his paper titled 'Dynamics of Transference' (1912), in which he elaborates that transference emanates from that portion of libidinal impulses that have remained unexpressed or unconscious. The dynamics of transference that present themselves in the process of analysis, are equally present outside this process as well. However, in analysis, these dynamics are made the object of study. It thus poses a challenge to treatment and also offers the strongest weapon of resistance. Transference can be a positive, affectionate type, which is an ally of the work, or erotic type which needs interpretive resolution. It can also be negative, posing much difficulty to the success of treatment. Freud's understanding was that the patient gets insight into how transference-based wishes fit into the 'nexus of treatment and his life history'; this process frees him/her from a tendency to re-create such situations. There was a turning point in Freud's understanding of transference, however, which was elaborated in *Beyond the Pleasure Principle* (1920). Here he noted that transference stemmed from a compulsion to repeat, that didn't always come in the service of the dominion of the pleasure principle, but this compulsive repetition at certain times, was in the service of unpleasure. Here he postulated the importance of the death drive in understanding this mutation of the transference.

At present, transference is considered a necessary construct in psychoanalytically oriented therapy. Working through transference helps facilitate the process of recovery for the patient. Instead of shying away from the emergence of transference, therapists now attempt to develop *transference neurosis,* so that the patient can play out their infantile conflicts with the therapist in an attempt to recreate them, gain awareness, and subsequently gain control of what, till now, had remained unconscious.

The term *transference neurosis* was coined by Carl Jung (1907); it implied a *psychoneurosis* which was caused by childhood psychological trauma. In transference neurosis, the libido is readily displaceable, and the possibility of developing transference existed. Freud (1914g) elaborated in connection with the observation that the patient repeats his or her infantile conflicts within the transference. He stated that 'we succeed in giving all the symptoms of the illness, a new transference meaning, and in replacing the patient's ordinary neurosis by a transference neurosis of which he can be cured during clinical work.'

Clinical work thus involves the resolution of transference neurosis by means of interpretation and working through. Once transference neurosis has been established, the therapist attempts to interpret this transference in order to gain insight into the patient's psyche and work through these conflicts to facilitate the patient's treatment.

Transference interpretation is the term for the therapist's intervention directed at unmasking the transference basis of a particular attitude, feeling, fantasy, or behaviour of the analysand. Freud (1912b) and later James Strachey (1934) emphasized that the truly mutative interpretations were the ones which have a sense of *immediacy* and credibility, owing to their pointing out the transference experience. Otto Fenichels (1941) makes a distinction between transference interpretation, which is 'the feeling you are actually having towards me, is actually directed towards your father', and 'reverse transference interpretation,' in which 'you are not feeling this about your father at this moment, but about me'. Merton Gill (1979) pointed out that the resistance to the awareness of transference needs interpretation before the transference itself. Transference interpretation has evolved over psychoanalytic history and now according to Arnold Cooper (1987), 'our once straightforward historical understanding of transference interpretation has yielded to a more polymorphous and confusing modernistic view.'

Countertransference, as defined by the psychoanalytic dictionary, is a term coined by Sigmund Freud (1910d) to describe the feelings generated in the analyst 'as a result of the patient's influence on the unconscious'. The classical view believed that counter transference was a serious hindrance to the treatment process, but an increasing number of analysts (Winnicott 1947; Heimann 1950; Racker 1953) began to observe the data of counter transference as useful information regarding the patient and what exactly was going on in the therapeutic process. Donald Winnicott (1949) demarcated an *objective counter-transference* which includes 'the analyst's love and hate in reaction to the actual personality and behaviour of the patient, based on objective observation'. He emphasized the significance of Hate in the counter-transference as a developmental milestone in working with psychotic patients, as his sense was that 'patients in analysis cannot be expected to tolerate his hate of the analyst unless the analyst can hate him'. This interpretation has to be made with the most careful timing, at a point when it can be tolerated by the patient.

Paula Heimann (1950) extended the concept of countertransference to include 'all feelings that the analyst experiences through the analytic session'. She liberated the concept of countertransference from negative connotations, placing it at the centre of the psycho-analytic technique. Heinrich Racker (1953, 1957, 1958) broke the monolithic notion of countertransference by classifying it into *direct*, which refers to the analyst's emotional response to the patient, and *indirect*, which refers to the analyst's emotional response to something important to the patient. Direct countertransference has two sub-categories: *concordant countertransference*, which implies the analyst's empathetic resonance with the patient's felt conflicts and is more marked if the analyst has had similar conflicts; and *complementary countertransference*, which refers to the analyst's unconscious identification with some unfelt or projected part of the patient's psychic structure, indicating that the analyst's emotional experience, in this case, was opposed to that of the patient. Other considerations in regard to the phenomenology of counter transference include its *intensity* (from mild to severe), *duration* (acute to chronic), and *clinical visibility* (gross or subtle).

The development of the relational and intersubjective perspectives have led to an understanding that both transference and countertransference are essentially a co-created phenomena. Through this, the notion of the 'neutral' analyst has also changed. Peter Givocchini (1989) in *Countertransference Triumphs and Catastrophes* explains that neutrality implies that you weigh each part of the psyche of the patient equally. It does not, however, indicate that you are entirely detached and non-emotional, which was initially considered a prerequisite for being an analyst. In this process, it stands to reason that the analyst would make certain associations to what is presented by the patient, whether or not she makes them aware of it. Understanding these associations would help better understand the subject. Nancy McWilliams (1999) in her book *Psychoanalytic Case History Formulation*, emphasizes the importance of paying attention to countertransference in assessing the patient. For example, analysts have reported feeling confused and all over the place, while in conversation with an individual in a manic state. Such insight, into our own feelings and responses, helps one diagnose, while also making the therapist aware of what kind of psychopathologies they can or cannot work with.

These examples indicate the presence of a dialectical between transference and countertransference.

There has also been a shift in the degree to which *countertransference enactment* is deemed inevitable. Ideally, the therapist should be able to monitor his/her affective responses to the patient, and dip into them to learn more about them, himself/herself, and the analytic process. More often the therapist shows certain *role responsiveness* to the patient's externalizations and grasps the meaning of it analytically, only on a post hoc basis. A converse problem is the therapist's resistance to feeling strained affects in the clinical situation (Coen 2002), and thus becoming unable to analyse the patient's material in its verity and depth. Here, one can see the significance of paying attention to countertransference as a way of better understanding the processes taking place in the *analytic association*. The involvement of real-life issues with countertransference (Slakter 1987), and of cultural differences (Akhtar 1999b) have also gained significance. What remains of utmost importance is the therapist's ability to feel a wide range of affects and fantasies in the clinical situation, and to apply his/her analytic thinking to these psychic productions of his/her own.

The understanding, and the use of the transference-countertransference matrix, is a significant part of psychoanalytically informed work. In my work in the clinic, especially with suicidal patients, I encountered a host of feelings and enactments: from feeling helpless and confused, to the anticipation of something opening up. Across the cases, it was important to provide a space to talk about these preoccupations and thoughts, so that the underlying feelings could be brought to the forefront. I noted that this was always difficult for the subject—talking about their suicidal thoughts came with as much trepidation as talking about a history of violence or being abused. A part of the task became providing a space to externalize these preoccupations and thoughts. In most cases, this was a first-time experience, and being able to tolerate and live that with them was, in my understanding, the strength of our analytic association.

As the work continued, what gained significance in my mind, was the roles I was being drawn into, and the positions that I occupied, within these dynamics. They carried a character particular to me, but established themselves in a position of otherness to the subject. Though these were not roles I identified with, they could at moments, be used in order to demarcate and identify a position of otherness. While working with C who identified as Muslim, elements of my Hindu identity were brought to the forefront. In my work with X who struggled with diagnosed mental illness, the absence of significant mental distress in my life history was identified. During my brief work with P, my being 'upper caste' was highlighted. Though my experience of these signifiers is more fluid, in the dynamic with the subject they would produce themselves in opposition, and often made me think about the difficult question of my own location and what that was doing to the subject. More than who I was, or what position I occupied, the perception of it being different, away from the position the subject was in, presented itself as significant in our interactions. In these moments, this otherness would highlight the limit of my own thinkability and location. Though something affective about these moments could be grasped and worked with, there remained something unknowable, experientially distinct from where I was located. My only recourse, in these moments, would be to rely on images of affective resonance, or reflection on the nature of this use of otherness, while constantly holding on to the idea that there was an otherness present here that could not be brought into assimilation easily.

Nature of the Sample

It is important to specify that the subjects that I worked with in the clinic were between the ages of 17 and 24 years. These subjects represented a tussle with identity formation, to the effect that identity had not become a stable structure, but was in the process of being created and found. These tussles and struggles with identity formation remained important to the work, as the subject attempted to negotiate between a sense of self that they carried from their history, and a sense of self that was in the process of being constructed. It would present itself in a manner that seemed reminiscent of an adolescent stage, where a negotiation with boundaries, the role of the body, and a sense of identity would become important. There were moments where I would feel close to, and identify deeply with, these struggles, having negotiated some of these quite recently myself, while still grappling with some of them, in my own process of identity development.

Adolescence and its Presentations

Adolescence, as a stage, gained salience as psychoanalysis progressed as a discipline. In earlier works, greater significance was given to infantile sexual development, especially with the publication of Freud's 'Three Essays of Sexuality' (1905). The infant as polymorphous perverse was an important development in this paper, which further highlighted the importance of the early stages in the development of sexuality. It took a while before psychoanalysis could attempt to turn to adolescence, which possibly required a movement from an intrapsychic model to a more relational understanding. Adolescence, as a stage, coincides with puberty. As a result of the biological changes that reach their height during this stage, there could be difficulty in gaining a sense of one's growing sexuality, and bringing that into representation. Adolescence then becomes a stage of negotiations, where the awareness of the self and the other are put into a different kind of crisis, with the awareness that one is now a sexual being.

Anna Freud (1958) looks at adolescence as the 'stepchild of psychoanalytic theory' and describes it as a stage similar to unhappy love affairs or periods of mourning. 'In both these latter states there is much mental suffering and, as a rule, the urgent wish to be helped; in spite of this, neither state answers well to analytic therapy' (Freud 1958) Perhaps, this urge to be helped, and this urgency, would communicate itself through bringing the subject to the clinic. It becomes important to think about how one works with the adolescent? Are these negotiations an attempt towards further psychic development? Her paper attempts to provide a set of instructions and guidelines, a kind of a warning about the difficulty of this state and the problems in working with it. She indicates that 'analytic treatment of adolescents is a hazardous venture from beginning to end' (ibid.) She qualifies this difficulty by indicating that adolescence is also a stage of great instability for the individual, such that the sense of self is constantly in flux. As a stage where identity formation takes on significance, certain technical difficulties may be experienced while working with adolescent patients. In her understanding, the adolescent's instability and rapid movements between subject positions, makes it difficult for the analyst to take stock of the situation and handle the case adequately. In Freud's understanding, in both unhappy love affairs and mourning, the libido is already invested in an object it cannot detach its preoccupation from; it becomes difficult for the adolescent to create or sustain a transference in analysis. On the contrary, there could also be a possibility of a certain kind of idealization of the analyst, where an infatuation develops, which could further act as an impediment to therapeutic work.

The relationship the university students have with the university as a space, and with the faculty as extensions of this space, can be thought about in this light. In my understanding, the subjects of the clinic appeared to be representing different parts of adolescence as a state, which Freud makes us aware of. There seems to be an idealization of the space provided in the university, in which is also expressed the desire for a holding and nurturant environment—a coexistence of transformative pedagogy, with an ethics of care. The university provides a space for dialogue, critical thinking, and dissent. At the same time, the presence of a clinic within the university could represent the bringing together of critique and care. The nature of transformative pedagogy is to evoke self-reflection, which can be experienced as a moment of crisis. In the narrations of the students, it would appear that a certain kind of fusion with the environment is fostered, where feelings of deep connection and isolation are negotiated simultaneously. There are breakdowns in public spaces, which are given a space, and there is a movement among students to actually seek psychotherapy. In the therapeutic encounters with these students, my sense is that they struggle to find a voice that is uniquely their own. In these moments, the therapist either becomes a facilitating presence or an attacking one that muffles the voice. The alternations happen so quickly, and the best recourse for the therapist in these instances is to just be present, and make the subject aware of the dynamics, as and when it is possible. It could also be postulated, that the university, in this sense, encourages adolescent states, because it provides the fantasy of sexuality that is contained in a liberal manner. Exploration of one's sexuality and preferences is given a space in the university in contrast to schools, where a budding sense of sexuality is curtailed with the threat of punitive measures. Given this transition and development from school to college, I began to wonder, *what kind of scaffold does the adolescent need for exploration and who is able to provide that space?*

Adam Phillips (1993), in his understanding of adolescence, takes us towards a different task in this stage. For him, the task of adolescence is to 'inhabit and be inhabited by the body' (1993, p. 31). Using Winnicott and Klein as his theoretical base, Phillips indicates that this is a stage where an individual puts their primary holding environment (the body) at risk, in an attempt to develop both a capacity for solitude and for concern. These capacities 'recapitulates something of infancy in a dramatically modified form' (ibid., p. 33). Thus, adolescence serves as a repetition and a reworking of what has been experienced as waiting, love, justice, concern, and quietude in the stages before.

Unlike Anna Freud's paper, which attempts to be more concrete in its imagination of adolescence and the difficulty of working with adolescents, Phillips tries to take us closest to the adolescent's inner world. He constructs it not as a conflict of drives that have a tenuous relationship with the object, but instead describes it as a stage of inherent paradoxes. 'One of the central paradoxes for the adolescent is his discovery that only the object beyond his control can be found to be reliable' (ibid., p. 30). In Winnicott's schema, the capacity to be alone is born out of the presence of the mother, similarly the capacity for solitude develops in relation to the body. The body occupies 'a special position among other objects in the world of perception' (Freud 1923, p. 3959).

Freud (1923), in his paper 'ego and the Id', foregrounds the importance of the body as a space, where the function of the ego is imbedded. He indicates that the ego is first and foremost a bodily one. To know one's body, and to feel its presence, Freud highlights the importance of touch and pain. In working in the clinic, I would wonder if the paradox that Phillips (1993) talks about could be understood from a structural perspective? To establish the function of reality testing, to know the limit of the self, the adolescent then risks the body. *Could this risk-taking extend beyond the thrill, and also be an exploration of the nature of this object, its capacity to hold, on one side, and as an intermediary between what is internal and what is external, on the other? How would this help us understand suicidality, which seems to be presenting itself in a similar stage?*

If the adolescent doesn't feel conscious of the body, has the adolescent lost something? If this body, which one is establishing a relationship with, isn't greeted with love and attraction, what kinds of effects would it have on the body and the psyche? If the body has the capacity to house solitude, it could also house shame, anger, hatred, disgust; could a 'generous kind of negligence' (ibid., p. 30) be necessary to understand what later becomes eating disorders and extreme body modification? *Could adolescence be postulated, as a stage, as a re-negotiation of the pleasure-pain principles as well? Could a preoccupation with suicidality be a signification of the same?*

The adolescent dilemma, of what to do and what not to do, is represented in the contrast Phillips draws between Klein and Winnicott. While Kleinian theory postulates a concern for the other as integral to a good life, Winnicott's development theory is more contingent on 'the capacity to relinquish or suspend concern for the object' (ibid., p. 33). Concern could be a compliant response to the environment, resulting in a false self-constellation. In emphasizing the mother's role and 'capacity to survive the instinctual moment, and so as to be there to receive and understand the true reparative gesture' (ibid., p. 36), he also seems to be alerting us to what kind presence, and capacities, the authorities that interact with adolescents could be open to embodying, in an attempt to facilitate non-compliant concern. An understanding of adolescence as a stage, in this manner, has facilitated work with subjects of the clinic, *in an attempt to further understand what can be provided by the clinic as a space, within the university as a structure.*

Identity and its Crisis

A large part of Erik H. Erikson's work brings together adolescence, as a life stage, and its relationship to what he describes as *identity crisis*. He writes that 'adolescence is a stage in which the individual is much closer to historical day than he is at earlier stages of childhood development' (1968, p. 27). Though developmentally adolescence is marked by the coming in of genitality, Erikson opens up an exploration of adolescence beyond an age specificity. He states,

> as technological advances put more and more time between early school life and the young person's final access to specialized work, the stage of adolescing becomes an even more marked and conscious period and, as it has always been in some cultures in some periods, almost a way of life between childhood and adulthood (ibid., p. 128).

Since the university offers a space of skill advancement, prior or parallel to the development of a specialized skill set, it might help us to understand the subjects of the university clinic as closer to what Erikson is describing as a *marked* and *conscious* period of adolescence. This adolescence is marked by a sense of identity confusion and crisis such that it is a 'necessary turning point, a crucial moment, when development must move one way or another, marshalling resources of growth recovery and further differentiation' (ibid., p. 16). In this crisis, the milieu of childhood gets replaced with that of society, which requires a 'moratorium for the integration of the identity elements' (ibid., p. 128). In the process of the integration of identity, the adolescent looks for opportunities to decide with freer assent, yet remains afraid of self-doubt or exposure to ridicule. There appears to be a willingness to put trust in people with an imagination and avoid that which seems pedantic.

Erikson (1968) elaborates that in the midst of the identity crisis, the adolescent attempts to be negotiating who they think they are and what others think they might be. He writes,

> They are sometimes morbidly, often curiously, preoccupied with what they appear to be in the eyes of others as compared with what

they feel they are, and with the question of how to connect the roles and skills cultivated earlier with the idea prototypes of today (ibid., p. 128).

Perhaps, this is what brings the subject of this preoccupation closer to the historical times they are imbedded in, since those prototypes themselves will be derivations of the social milieu at the time of the identity crisis. While working with students from the university, I was faced with a lot of identity confusion that was being communicated at different stages. With undergraduate students, it seemed closer to an attempt to bring together the context they had grown up in, with the pedagogy the university exposed them to. This was still closer to a sense of finding a footing in a ground that felt unfamiliar. With postgraduate students, it presented itself in a question: *what is my stance on a particular situation?* These stances were usually around a dominant ideology, and their attempt was to understand the impact of their stance, on themselves and those around them.

In my work in the clinic, I began to wonder, can an identity crisis predicate a kind of suicidality, when elements of identity formation become too conflicting? When it came to preserving a part of what felt like a possible identity element, I noted that there were many things the subject was willing to do or completely unwilling to do, no matter what the consequences. As a sense of developing into an ethical subject seemed to be underway, some were preoccupied with the value they could add to the society, what their subject positions meant, what they were being taught, and how it could be used. They reflected upon the politics within the university and sometimes experienced a sense of fear of being a particular marginalized identity in the current socio-political climate. To diagnose these moments as borderline or narcissistic would only address part of the question. These moments seemed to be a negotiation with very real and current themes within the social milieu, which required a space to be thought about and communicated. *I have wondered what moments like these, within the clinical space, tell us about the social milieu we inhabit? Could this identity crisis help us understand something about the rise in suicide rates amongst the youth? What would suicidality look like in the face of an identity crisis? If we follow on from Erikson's hypothesis, what about our historical moment is being represented in the life histories and crises that enter the clinic?*

Inside/Out Outside/In: Towards a Psychosocial Understanding

Though the role of the socio-political context has always retained a significance in my mind, it remained difficult to process it completely while working with the subjects of the clinic. To understand it in a fuller sense, I had to write out the case histories and reflect on individual moments where these came to the forefront. While the work was ongoing, the primary concern remained the distress, discomfort, and preoccupations the patient brought in. I realized that I could only return to some of the questions within this research once the work with the patient was over, or had at least reached some stage of completion. Possibly, this would allude to my difficulty in using my work in the clinic for the purpose of this research. It, thus, becomes important to state that some of these directions could only be returned to once the work was terminated, and I was freer to think beyond the communication and enactments of suicidality. This allowed for a dialectic between understanding patienthood and reflecting on subject positions, for the purpose of this research. It also highlighted for me the difficulty of working with suicidality within the university clinic, which will be elaborated on in later chapters.

While reflecting on the work with the subject at the clinic, the importance of the social milieu the subject and I were embedded in, along with the specificities of our life histories, emerged to the forefront. In an attempt to understand this better, I began to wonder about the multiple positions at play in the moments of transference, when two life histories and personalities came together, with their constellation of communities and subject positions, within a space with its own specificity of location; within a university, which at present is fraught with turbulence.

Clinical work and experience has maintained a relationship with larger social factors at play in the production of a symptom and its maintenance, sometimes in a more direct and involved manner, sometimes in a peripheral manner. The role of the 'environment' is attributed significance in the development of the psyche, and different elements of this environment have been foregrounded by different thinkers, at different times. This has not only allowed us to understand the nature of intrapsychic processes, but interpsychic as well, along with their impact on the constitution of the subject, and the role they play in healthy development and symptom formation.

Freud's work has often been charged with addressing 'an unrepresented minority of the respectable bourgeois and well to do' (Rose 2004, p. vii). His later work, however, attempts to explore the interplay of the Id, ego, and ego Ideal that constitute the individual psyche and their interaction with larger social environments they are constituted in/with. Jaqueline Rose (2004) indicates that for Freud, mental life cannot exist without the presence of the other. As also seen in the formulation of the ego Ideal, the psyche is always in interaction with that which is outside it. Through the process of identification, Rose points out that, 'we only exist through others who make up the storehouse of the mind: models in our first tentative steps towards identity, objects of our desires, helpers and foes' (2004, p. vii). Rose argues that a lot of Freud's preoccupations came from the time he was historically located in, between the first and second world wars. The rise of anti-Semitic sentiments across Europe, and the loss of reason were his preoccupations, reflected in the nature of symptoms he worked with. He seemed to be preoccupied with the nature of hatred and violence, and what makes it possible on a larger collective level. In 'Mass Psychology and the Analysis of the I' (1920, p.17),[2] he begins by stating that individual psychology is of course directed at the person in isolation, tracing the ways in which he seeks to satisfy his drive impulses, but only rarely, in specific exceptions, is it able to disregard the relationship between the individual and others. In an attempt to understand this relationship, Freud looks at the institution of the church and the army, exploring the nature of identifications and

[2] Translated as *Group Psychology and the Analysis of the ego* in the Standard Edition.

idealizations that are made possible in each mass, and how that mass comes to function as a collection of individuals, creating a whole. What he seems to be foregrounding here, is not just what draws the particular individual to a mass, but also how the larger mass creates its own history and constellation, such that the individual 'I' is no longer at the forefront. The mass then, has an agency of its own and is capable of feats that were impossible for the individual alone. In choosing the church and the army, I believe Freud is also commenting on what kind of subject positions and masses become important in a particular historical context, though this seems to be an unconscious thread in his writing.

More directly, Erik Erikson (1968) attempts a careful revision of the idea of the subject as only projecting infantile conflicts onto the external world, different alone and different in the group. Building on Freud, he states 'contemporary social models are both clinically and theoretically relevant and cannot be shunted off by brief and patronizing tributes to the role "also" played by "social factors"' (1968, p. 45). Using Freud, he reiterates that the ego finds itself between the biological Id and the sociological masses. These sociological masses exert restrictions on the ego, through the critical influence of parents, professional educators, and those who make up milieu and public opinion. Reflecting on his clinical work, in the developmental movement from self-love to self-esteem, he found that there remains 'the constructive necessity of social organization in the individual's development' (ibid., p. 47). To elaborate on this, he proposes *Ego Identity,* the 'subjective aspect, in the awareness of the fact that there is a self-sameness and continuity to the ego's synthesizing methods, the style of one's individuality, and that this style coincides with the sameness and continuity of ones meaning for significant others in the immediate community' (ibid., p. 50). Ego identity is, however, different from personal identity, which is based on a perception of self-sameness and continuity within the individual—which emerges post identity crisis and confusion—and the fact that others in the community recognize it.

Erikson foregrounds the significance of the social milieu and the socio-political context the subject is present in by looking at the possibilities of identifications and the roles made available at a given time, within a given community. He states, 'the historical era in which he [the subject] lives, offers only a limited number of socially meaningful models for workable combinations of identification fragments' (ibid., p. 53). The social then, becomes an important factor, not just in the constitution of the subject, but also in the position made available for the subject to occupy. By looking at the youth of the time, along with subjects of the clinic, Erikson draws a link between the historical violence of post-war migration and the development of new systems of democracy and freedom with particular emphasis on its manifestation on the youth. He does so not in an attempt to label or pathologize the youth, but to highlight the significance of adolescence, as a stage, signifying a representation of contemporary crisis, through a tussle with identity. For Erikson (1968), 'To discuss the identity problem, then, and to describe its dimensions at the very time when we clinicians are listened to, means to play into cultural history, or perhaps, to become its tool' (p. 27).

The social milieu of the subject, the nature of meaningful models of identification, and the confusions around identity were evident/ important/significant in the subjects I was working with, along with a preoccupation with suicidality. *I wonder whether a contemporary crisis is being represented in this symptom, in individual life histories?* Further the question becomes, *how does one understand, analyse, or interpret material from the clinic, to decipher what it tells us about the construction of the subject, without reducing this analysis to something simply intrapsychic in nature?*

Bringing together these questions becomes structurally difficult at times. However, it is here that a turn towards a psychosocial understanding becomes helpful in holding together the different parts of the research question. As I began to think about the work in the clinic, I also began to reflect on my own subject position, with its own struggles with identity elements, that came to the forefront in the course of working within a university clinic. The tussle that felt most significant to my position was navigating an ethics of care for the other, while also negotiating a sense of self that could work with the social and political, along with the psychological. How to make psychotherapeutic work accessible and understandable beyond the clinic remains an important preoccupation. To retain elements of a clinical sensibility, while also coming to my own sense of a political identity, still feels like a struggle in process; I remain unaware of its edges and curves, but reflection on the same remains a continuous thread in my writing. *To think about the nature of crisis, as reflected by the subject of the clinic then, also becomes a moment of reflection on my own states of crisis, as a subject within the university as a space.*

There were many cases that could have been considered possible subjects for this work, given their preoccupations with taking their lives and/or their locations as students within the university. It would be important to clarify why the three cases of C, X and P were chosen in particular, to elaborate this work. On one level, choosing C and X as subjects comes from having engaged with them for the longest amount of time, during my training. Both C and X have been 'long-term cases', defined by the tenure of the work we were able to do together, and the comparative sense of depth and understanding that I was able to reach while working with them. More specifically, C has been the first suicidal patient I worked with. From the beginning of therapy, to its pause, to resuming work, till a final termination, C remained an important patient in my mind. She was the first. My work with her helps elaborate my own struggles while beginning work with suicidality, the questions that came from the same, along with my own concerns and preoccupations with the construct.

By the time I began working with X, I had already been working with suicidal patients and emergency cases. Though there was some degree of familiarity with the same therefore, X's presentation of his suicidality struck me as unique in itself. While working with him, I began to think more fully about the difficulty of working with this presentation of suicidality, and its impact on the therapist. I became more aware of my own affect states; at moments carrying a deep sense of anxiety about his actions, at others, a deep sense of hope at his ability to still seek help. I also became more aware of my desire to attend to these movements within him and in other patients as well. Given that

X was the most articulate about his plans and desires to end his life, he occupied, at moments, a position of centrality in supervisory processes and my own thinking as well. Reflecting on the work with him becomes important to the present research, therefore, not just to highlight the movements within the dyad, but also to think about the kind of position these subjects they occupied within my mind in the therapeutic process.

In the initial conception of the research, I had intended to add a section of vignettes of my work with younger undergraduate students, in an attempt to reflect upon their experience of both the university and the clinic, highlighting their struggles between the two spaces, and the nature of their identity crisis, that at times presented itself as suicidal symptoms. This section however has now become a reflection on P's case, as a result of his death by suicide. For me, P's death by suicide becomes a representation of a crisis and struggle, which becomes important to talk about and think about, not just for the part of me that has been a trainee in this university clinic, in which P had come in as a patient, but also for that part of me, which remained a student within the university space, concerned by the rise of such cases within this space in our current socio-political climate.

While bringing together C, X and P's cases, I also began to realize that there was more to choosing these three than what I have already indicated. In these three cases in particular, each subject occupied a location of social otherness, and while working with each of them, this location of otherness expressed itself within the dynamics of transference. *An otherness representing a quality or a state of being different, at moments presenting a possibility for further exploration and elaboration of this difference, at others presenting a collapse of conversation, carrying a quality of unknowability.* In working with C, markers of my Hindu identity became other to the Muslim parts she was beginning to identify with. In working with X, a relationship with otherness was established due to my privilege of not having prolonged exposure to mental illness and violence, as he did within his family. In my work with P, my upper caste location constructed an otherness to his location of being Dalit. This otherness seemed also to establish itself with identity elements that I am yet to assimilate and own. It also appeared that as the work continued, these were identity elements C, P, and X were grappling with as well. It is in reflecting on these moments, that I became more aware of the complex nature of the dynamics of transference and countertransference between two subjects, with a shared historical context, close to the same life stage.

This dialogue between these two subject positions, in crisis, and in moments towards resolution, has been represented in a case presentation format in the present work. The attempt of this representation is not just to present a patienthood, but also to understand the nature of suicidality, its interplay with identity elements within the subject's psyche, while also reflecting on the analytic association with the therapist, who also remains a subject in crisis.

The methodology then, includes psychoanalytically informed psychotherapy, which moves towards a psychosocial understanding of the subject, the field, and the spaces of the university and the clinic.

CHAPTER 3

Attempts at Engagement
Case Representations

C's Case

C, a 25-year-old female, was the first 'suicidal' patient I worked with in the clinic. Our work spanned over a year and three months, during which time she terminated therapy and resumed again amid some important life transitions. C's 'suicidal thoughts' did not present themselves in a linear manner, as a preoccupation in thought, or in the shape of activities that would be considered life-threatening. Her *suicidality* became apparent in situations that were potentially dangerous to her sense of self. She repeatedly got involved in relationships that threatened her developing yet shaky sense of self, despite a rising awareness about the same. In these moments, it would be difficult for her to pause and reflect; something about dealing with affect became too intolerable and acting out seemed to be the only way for her to regain a semblance of her sense of self, no matter what the cost. Intimacy of any kind became a difficult terrain to navigate while also becoming a representation of the internal confusions she carried around regarding her sense of identity—what it meant to be a free-thinking liberal woman on the one hand, and what it meant to be a 'good' Muslim on the other.

As she continued to be in therapy, a part of her allied with the free-thinking liberal woman she found in me, while another part remained suspicious. This part believed that I could not possibly understand her subject position because I came from a different community. Parallel to this, she moved from feeling like she had no space within her family, to opening up channels of communication with other women within the family, especially her mother and her aunt. Through the confusions she struggled with, she seemed to have found a way to return to a sense of identity within the community. Despite the difficulties this precipitated, the return to a relational identity remained a more significant desire within her.

In my work with C, I began to think of how suicidality presents itself, not just in ideation but in forms and patterns, networks of signification, and around repetitive patterns that are not entirely outside the subject's awareness. Despite this awareness, these patterns have a pervasive hold within the psyche. Could an understanding of these patterns help us get a clearer sense of C's 'suicidal thoughts' and what they began to represent for her?

From the Referral Form to the Clinic: Beginnings

When C's form was assigned to me, I was struck by her name. I had never heard it before. As she had indicated a specific date to be contacted by, I had time to sit with her form before contact was initiated. Her reasons for referral sounded urgent, yet there was a poised calm in the writing, as if trying to maintain a sense of semblance amidst chaos.

She wrote,

> I am having difficulty dealing with my current life status. Though I try real hard to be okay, but when I break down it comes to the point of having suicidal thoughts. It's like a cycle of highs and lows. Given the repetitive break downs, my own attempts to help myself don't seem to be working. I want a permanent end to this

cycle. I was working before and I left my job amidst a personal life crisis. I have in past visited a private psychologist who said that I was suffering from clinical depression. This is one year back. I did not continue with her therapy as it was difficult for me to open up and trust people in my situation. Things are a little better since then, but gets really difficult sometimes.

This was the first form I had received with the term 'suicidal thoughts' in it and *that* was the first thing that caught my attention. I wondered about her repetitive patterns and her feelings of breakdown. I was surprised when I discovered that she contacted the clinic prior to the date mentioned on her form, conveying a sense of urgency. I called her immediately and a soft urgent voice on the other end of the line asked for the earliest appointment that I could give so we decided to meet three days later.

That was a chaotic morning for the clinic as the key to the door that opens into the corridor had been lost. As the guards gathered to assess their options, I wondered about mine. Should I reschedule the session? Should I give extra time depending on whether they manage to open the door? Was the next slot free? All these questions raced through my mind as the guards grew more anxious due to my presence. Eventually they managed to break the lock without harming the door. It was quite a victory for them and I also felt relieved as C hadn't yet arrived. I soon began to wonder if she would come at all. Twenty-five minutes into the appointment, I messaged her asking if she would be coming for the session. As I awaited her response, many thoughts went through my mind. I wondered if everything was alright. If she knew the way to the clinic, maybe she had got lost; but in that case wouldn't she call or check in? Should I call? I didn't hear from her till the last five minutes of the appointment. Her message read, 'I'm extremely sorry I won't be able to come today. Probably I will take a consultation for later. Thanks a lot.'

I was a little stumped; possibly a little irritated as well, but I didn't have access to that feeling, at that point. I went back to her referral form and thought about her repetitive patterns, her suicidal thoughts.

I thought about her urgency to come and her writing in to the clinic. How does an enthusiastic person, who recognizes they need help, not show up for a first consultation? I had the option of not thinking about it any further, returning the form, and taking another, but this nagging feeling wouldn't leave me. She hadn't given a reason for why she was unable to come; maybe she had got caught in something? Maybe she had got nervous? I also found it difficult to ignore her voice, and the presence of the phrase 'suicidal thoughts' in the form. So, after a few days of thinking about it, I decided to leave her a message. That nagging feeling wouldn't leave me, so I thought to myself, if she doesn't respond, I will return the form, having given her the option to visit.

C responded positively to the message and agreed to come the following week. She was late for the session and as I messaged her again, she informed me that she was in the campus but unable to make it to the clinic yet. She was well groomed and looked well put together when she came in, until she started talking. She foregrounded a 'relationship issue' that she was currently preoccupied with. She described it as her 'first serious relationship', and despite the fact that she and her partner came from different communities (H was Hindu), she hoped it would culminate in marriage.

As she went on to describe the relationship, it was difficult to get a pulse on what had led her to H. They had broken up about a year ago as the relationship had become rather strained and was bordering on physical and mental abuse. Yet, she had remained preoccupied with repairing something there, so that marriage, as an option, could be revisited. Due to issues in this relationship, she was unable to concentrate on anything else and feared that her preparation for the upcoming competitive exams would be inadequate. It was difficult for me to get a sense of the significance of this relationship for her as it sounded rather toxic, yet her affective responses seemed to be speaking differently, with endearment and care. C's relationships and her career trajectories became important points of discussion in our work subsequently.

As this short session came to an end, and the necessary exchanges about structure and fee were completed, I felt the need to ask her why she had been unable to make it to the clinic last week. She smiled sheepishly and said, 'I actually came till CP[1] and decided to go back because I was in a good enough place so I didn't know what I would come and talk to you about here.' I was taken in by her honesty and told her that I had been wondering if she knew the way here, or had lost her way. She laughed loudly exclaiming that she could never get lost in Delhi. I laughed with her, while reminding her that I had had no way of knowing that about her! As we laughed towards the end of this session, I had a fleeting hope that we would be able to work together.

C was one of my long-term cases while working in the clinic. Throughout the time I worked with her, I have gone back to this series of events in my mind. Between her writing in about not being contacted and her turning back midway; between the clinic key being lost and the breaking of the lock while the door was intact; from my oscillating between returning the form and holding the slot, and her making it to CP and then finally making it to the clinic. Between urgency and absence, what becomes of the missed session? I have wondered about what prompted me to hold that slot and beyond that curiosity, the impact the term 'suicidal thoughts' had had on me.

The Milieu and Its Interaction: Between Trauma and Controversy

In our initial consultations, I felt I had to actively enquire to grasp C's history. She belonged to an elite Muslim family. She grew up in a joint family but eventually moved out of the house for higher education. From an early age she began to notice the differences in the rules for girls in the house and the set of rules extended to the boys. Due to this she experienced her family as conservative while also feeling that they had given her the opportunity to grow beyond this through her education. Being the eldest child in the family had, at moments, been difficult for her. She felt the need to set a precedent for the other children in the family. At other moments, she felt that

---

[1] Connaught place (CP) is located at a distance of 8 km from the Clinic, which indicated to me that she was almost more than halfway there when she turned back and decided not to come.

her father would have preferred it if she were a boy. She had two younger brothers and recalled the difference between how her mother responded to them in comparison to how she had been with her. She described herself as 'a typically defiant adolescent' and remembered having a difficult relationship with her mother. Though she always felt close to her father, as she grew older, the culturally sanctioned distance between them began to widen. Moving out of the house for higher studies helped her deal with these relationships better.

C would find it incredibly difficult to talk to me about her family. She felt I couldn't possibly understand most of what she was saying given that we came from such different cultures. She would feel rather embarrassed by some of her thoughts and gradually expressed her fears of being judged. It was as if, in these moments, not only was I judging her, but one community was judging the other. Despite that, she would attempt to bring to dialogue the conflicts in her mind. I think what aided this dialogue was a particular stance I took in the work—of never denying that our subjective locations were different. Her concern was as real as my desire to be present to it. I believe that this is what allowed us to talk about it. Parallel to this, was her relationship to H, who also didn't belong to her community, and that too was important. This relationship added to the fears she carried. Though she could see a link between this and her current distress, a part of her needed to stay close to her immediate concerns. Her primary focus was engaged with creating a routine that would enable her to prepare for her upcoming exams. It was important to do that simultaneously as it appeared that only when that was in place could any further exploration be made possible. We needed to create that outline. Something had to be put neatly in place before the messy parts could be addressed.

As a narrative of her experiences so far began to open up, I felt that in C's mind there was a collapse between trauma and its associated affect. She would recount traumatic events in a distant, affectless manner while constantly questioning 'why are we even talking about this?' These moments were prefixed with an uncertainty of whether something should be said or not and when she did manage to say it, she wanted to dismiss it instantly. Her fears of being judged resurfaced while also dismissing the impact these experiences might have had on her. I felt saddened as she talked about difficult encounters in her life, but what struck me more was her manner of narration. It was as though these experiences could not find space in conversation because of their controversial nature. Her narrations were governed by 'what will people think?' This unconsciously minimized the trauma she was marked by in that moment and the pain that came with it.

Intimacy and Identity: Splits between Good and Bad

C carried multiple confusions about intimacy and her body. In her experiments in intimacy, she had experienced the Muslim partners she had been with as conservative and judgemental. As a non-practising Muslim, she felt that her religious identity and her beliefs were constantly being called into question—'I was told I wasn't a good Muslim' —and questions around her own sexuality seemed to be fraught with anxiety. Any moment of sexual curiosity or expression was experienced as intrusive or excessive. That seemed to be the nature of sexuality and intimacy across her relationships: something unthinkable, unclean and unbearable. Instances with an erotic or intimate charge were narrated with a touch of disgust and anger. There seemed to be multiple things at stake but they constellated themselves around her attempts to formulate her identity. The question of what becomes of her desire became an important undercurrent in our work.

In her relationship with H, C would find moments of intimacy confusing. Despite being together for a considerable amount of time, any gestures towards intimacy would invoke disgust in C. Yet her insistence remained that since this was a serious relationship, it must end in marriage. The prospect of marriage seemed like an impossibility in itself, owing to the fact that H was a Hindu. While listening to her, I often wondered about her sense of urgency around the prospect of marriage. Though there wasn't any communicated pressure from the family, since they had always taken pride in her academic pursuits, the pressure seemed to be coming from 'the social notion of what women should be doing'. 'Let's face it,' she would say, 'I am reaching that age by which marriage needs to happen or it will be too late.'

Despite the difficulties with H, she still attempted to restore her relationship with him. She recounted how terribly affected she would be when she fought with him and how on one such occasion, her tongue went numb. She was at home at the time and this incident caused great anxiety for everyone at home. Things got better once the fight with H was resolved. What helped her deal with these experiences was becoming preoccupied with work. Hence, even in our work together, it was important for her to constantly create a routine for herself. At this point in our work, my understanding was that there were multiple buried emotions that were finding their way out, in one way or another. A part of me also felt the need to enable this part and empower it, so that she could access different versions of herself.

As she resumed conversation with H, the internal structures she had built broke down, but this time in a manner that caused some reflection. She felt that she had done a lot of unforgivable and impulsive things to the people she had been with earlier, and at moments, these things, in fact, could sound crazy. When she felt that H had been lying to her, she had contacted his mother and even his ex-girlfriend to corroborate what he had told her. Since the mother didn't know about their relationship, H was rather upset with this transgression, which only appeared to her as a transgression now. In the moment though, it was difficult for her to see beyond the experience of hurt she carried. She felt that she had been wronged because he had kept their relationship a secret and didn't want to marry her. It was as if her worst fears had been realized as there was some truth in this too. She used the session as a space for confession where she came out with all that she too had done, and was doing, in the process of maintaining and fixing this relationship. It was, however, difficult to pause and think through in those moments. She felt simultaneously a lot of anger and shame. There were multiple affects short circuiting in the room. Treating it like a confession, took it, once again, closer to an unspeakable conflict in her mind, dissociating once more the experience of trauma it carried.

Between Confession and Redemption: Attempts to Belong

Though the relationship with H didn't work out eventually, my sense was that this theme of confession and redemption occupied an important position in C's narrative. She began to develop a curiosity about the same. As the relationship with H came to an end, she resumed a sustained external focus on her upcoming exam. It was important for her to foreground the career trajectory that she intended to embark on. At the same time, she became curious about her psyche, trying to think through what these events had come to symbolize for her. Having gained support from her mother at a crucial point in her relationship with H, C felt that a relationship should be sought within the community. She couldn't imagine inflicting the same kind of grief on her parents and felt that she no longer had the internal resources to take on the other religion. As she gravitated towards another relationship, she felt the need to take it slow. K belonged to the same community as her, which felt helpful; yet C remained concerned about whether she would be able to give herself to this relationship. Though this confusion remained, it was also important for C to have an intimate other in her life. She was surprised at herself when she responded anxiously to K's affection. Physical intimacy of any kind became intimidating. She said, 'It feels bad. I don't like it. It always feels bad. And that has always been the case. I don't like it and it is not limited to this person. I just do not like it.' Though this wasn't a new feeling, she was beginning to see a pattern at this point.

C seemed conflicted between exploring her own sexuality and finding a legitimacy for it. In the absence of a clear external sanction in the form of marriage, her internal experience of these moments was fraught with great anxiety, a sense of violation, and at moments, abuse. As we talked about her new relationship with K, she shared that what she liked about it the most was the staggered contact. Due to his job that involved a lot of travelling, they had limited time together and that slowed down the pace in a manner that felt helpful to her. At a certain point she felt that she must confess to him all that had happened to her before she met K and as we explored this further, we came to a shared understanding of what she thought that would achieve. The interplay between confession and redemption seemed to be an important one in her mind, yet she found it absurd when it came in contact with the liberal parts of her identity. She struggled between opening up parts of her past to her present and feared the effect this would have on her future. Nonetheless, she also felt the need to own her narrative and wondered why she should have to bare/share it to begin with. This remained a tussle in C's mind, but had become a tolerable one. She decided to terminate work in an attempt to concentrate on her career and decided that she would return to therapy when she had more mental space to address these concerns.

The nature of repetition in C's life marked her in ways that was difficult to understand and even more difficult to tolerate. This pattern required a slow processing, yet it evoked something so primal that its only response could be seen in enactment. She resumed therapy at a point when she felt like she had gone into crisis. Being marked by her past experiences and the awareness of the same did not prevent their reoccurrence. There seemed to be something more powerful at play here and C returned in the hope to understand that.

In her relationship with K, her experience was that he had 'disappeared from the scene', once they had become intimate. After not hearing from him for a while, she found out that he was getting engaged to someone else. She felt extremely betrayed and heartbroken about this; marriage was a topic they had been actively discussing. She was constantly in tears and felt like her whole life was falling apart. She simultaneously felt enraged that she still hoped that things could get better with him, despite him saying, 'I will make your life miserable if we end up together.' It was difficult to imagine what had prompted K to make this statement. It seemed like quite a contrast from the sense of stability and maturity she had carried about him. In this narration, K sounded more and more like H and I wondered about how it got there.

When C heard about K's engagement, she called on K's landline and spoke to his mother and brother. The brother called her 'a loose charactered woman' and proclaimed he was well-aware of how big city girls are. This made C livid as she felt that she was the only one at the receiving end of the judgement of a premarital relationship. According to C, K's family comes from a middle-class background. 'Well they are orthodox Muslims and you know, they're also... well... not as affluent as my family.' K's mother felt that they must meet C's parents and try to find a way to deal with the matter. She felt that since her son had been involved with C, he should be held equally responsible. Premarital involvement in itself was a great sin and C shouldn't have to handle the repercussions of such an intimate relationship on her own.

C's experience was one of violation, but she wasn't unaware that this time, she had gone too far, to get what she wanted from the situation. We tried to reconstruct her relationship with her body once more, reflecting on the burden of abuse it carried. Together, we thought about how our work had also paused at a point where these things were becoming more and more apparent to her. C's sense of her own religious identity felt under attack as K's brother branded her 'a bad Muslim'. This wasn't the first time it had been said to her; she had heard it before and carried a pervasive experience of the same. At this juncture, being labelled a woman of loose character and a bad Muslim splintered her sense of self. The feelings of rejection were magnified, as a part of her simultaneously felt that these binaries were socially constructed and were limiting her. Yet, they felt all-pervasive and the desire to be a good Muslim woman felt so deep and desperate that it seemed like she would give anything to occupy that position.

C was in contact with K again and a lot more was about to unfold. K was furious about C's accusations and by this time, K's parents had called off his engagement. K's mother felt that K had brought shame to the family and the religion by being involved with a woman and committing to marry another. C indicated that K was violently enraged at C and had communicated an intent to make her suffer. C, on the other hand, appeared bewildered by the responses she was getting, being cast as victim and perpetrator simultaneously. Things started moving along further as meetings were set up between the families. There were talks about marriage and doubts about the same. C seemed indecisive, and her indecisiveness became more apparent in our sessions. It was as if, she wanted someone else to tell her that this was a right idea but no one seemed to be doing so. She grew more frustrated with therapy and with the fact that I wasn't suggesting what was right or wrong, but just made room for her feelings with her, which she experienced as irrelevant. An invitation to explore her own imagination of family dynamics was perceived as an attempt to make her sound bigoted. I was doing something to her, instead of helping her out and just agreeing. My own sense was of watching something disastrous unfurl. I feared for her safety and her life after marriage. At moments I felt defeated for the ambitious part in her that wanted to achieve so much more. I felt helpless and incapacitated to help her.

In our last session together, C shared that she had concluded that backing away from the proposal would bring great shame to the family since there were so many people involved and maybe this was the 'only way I can atone for what I have done in the past'. She felt like she was being punished and if she could live out this situation, with a family structure so different from hers, with a relationship to religion so different from the one she had been initiated into, she would be able to undo the sins she had committed. The compulsion to repeat rang clear in my mind, but I felt too helpless to help her confront it. I realized that she was unwilling to explore these parts of herself. Without her will, there was nothing I could do to make space for them, if she didn't want that. Any question or interpretation from my side was taken as a reminder that 'I don't like the way things are going either, and you reminding me just doesn't help.' Her stance was 'I know. I know what you're going to say but this is done and needs to be followed through now. It's the only way.'

There was something stoic in C on that last day and something that didn't want to be uncertain. Though there were so many things one could explore about her experience of identity—a sanctioning of sexuality, or the need for belonging or approval—my sense was that C had made up her mind. Therapy had been helpful to her and she felt grateful for it but she didn't want to come here and be reminded of what else was going on, internally. As she genuinely thanked me for making time to see her and all the help I had given, I felt overcome with sadness and concern.

The image in my mind was of watching someone stoically walk into a chamber of fire and it left me thinking, is there no other way?

On the Nature of Suicidality

If we think back to C's reasons for referral, her repetitive patterns and her desire to find a permanent end to them, one can see a movement in the process of therapy. The session becomes a space to reflect on the complexity of these patterns and their interactions with both life historical moments and the socio-political context she remains enmeshed in. For the purpose of this work, the nature and transition of the term 'suicidal thoughts' becomes significant. While talking about her adolescence, in the initial consultation period, she recounted having cut herself as a response to a fight with her mother. She couldn't remember the details of the fight, but carried the marks on her wrist. She was 13 at the time but never cut herself again. As she expanded on the nature of her suicidal thoughts, she felt she 'lacked the courage' that one required to actually commit the act. She had never attempted to take her life, but at times she contemplated it. The image she would evoke was one of drowning in a large expansive body of water, though she knew how to swim. She felt that this was a painless way to die. On hearing this, I thought about the choice, knowing how painful drowning can be, and about how she was possibly holding on to that choice as she knew how to swim. I also wondered about the kind of pain she was in, and its impact on her body. In C's case, her suicidal thoughts and their interplay seemed to manifest on her body, in cutting and in drowning.

Though one can articulate a suicidal thought, how 'suicidality', as a feeling, communicates itself became important in this case. The desire for a serious relationship to culminate in marriage, no matter what the cost, could be seen as a tendency to move towards a resolution, not devoid of its punishing character. In C's case though, there wasn't conscious articulation of the nature of suicidal thoughts; what became salient was the texture of suicidality as a feeling. In the latter part of our work together, it presented itself in her desire to not feel anything: 'I want the feelings to stop'. Between communication and its breakdown, C seemed to be negotiating a tendency towards committing an act. An act that carried a potentially destructive charge, putting to risk other parts of herself. She could see no other way, which is what was significant and communicated most closely the despair created. However, the act of marriage, despite its proximity to suicidality, with possible attacks on significant parts of her-self, also seemed to be an act through which she stood a chance to atone, to return to her imagination of community, and regain a sense of belongingness. This could possibly be why this was a risk she was willing to take.

C's suicidality represented itself through conflicts between identity elements that were difficult to bring together. Her experience of what it meant to be a woman was marked by multiple absences, which remained difficult for her to return to: creating a play between active and passive, between being able to do for the self and having it done to the self, at times with a tone of harshness towards her intimate relationships and partners. She looked at these relationships with a strong sense of judgement, which at momentarily became confessionary, when she brought it to the clinic. In her narrative, there seemed to be a collapse between trauma and controversy, such that, that which was experienced as traumatic also carried a shade of being controversial—a controversy that she possibly felt she had some active (though unconscious) role in creating. There remained a hope for some reconciliation in her mind, in each case, with H and with K. I wondered how this reconciliation was reflective of the position her critical agency had come to occupy. Though it was difficult for her to understand or reflect on her own role in these relationships, C also carried the sense that she had to fix them, keep them together, at moments despite herself. It seemed to me that these were also the instances where C occupied a more active role, through confession, in the hope of redemption. Reflecting on things, waiting for them to unfurl, or giving them time carried a passivity which seemed to be too difficult for her to bear.

C carried a very strong imagination of what was right and what was wrong, what was good and what was bad. These positions, however, did not interact with each other and represented themselves the most in her struggles around being Muslim. To be a woman in this context can, in itself, be an experience of otherness. For C, attempts to identify with a community that has had a long experience of being and feeling othered, brought with it a complexity, which to a great extent had to be split. The liberal woman and the devout Muslim daughter could not seem to reconcile with each other. These positions don't render themselves occupiable very easily. Though C was the firstborn on her father's side of the family, she carried the sense that 'he always wanted a son'. It was difficult for her to talk about this, and it appeared that her mother was also absorbed by the same. When C's brothers were born six to seven years later, she noted a marked difference in her mother's interaction with them, and what had been her interaction with C until then. Her mother remained a passive figure in C's narrative and only appeared in an active form when C began exploring her experience of adolescence. Her adolescence was marked by a dramatic shift in how she was to conduct herself at home, especially around her father. She felt a distance from him at this point, a distance that she still carried; even now, as a woman in the bloom of her youth. C seemed troubled while talking to me about these experiences, fearing 'a sense of judgement because we belong from different communities'. Though there was truth in such apprehension, there was also truth in this being an experience most girls have to navigate within our culture, whatever the community they belong to; subsequently, the permissible intimacy between the father and the daughter, and what that intimacy translates into, for her, became an important point of reflection in our work.

C described a 'craving for love' which she had gone looking for in her intimate relationships, in the absence of finding a space for it in her immediate familial environment. This craving for love seemed so strong that, at moments, she was willing to sustain a great deal of unpleasure in the hope that this craving would be satisfied, eventually. This highlighted itself in instances where she would minimize herself as a working professional woman, in the hope of maintaining a relationship with H. It appeared again in her relationship with K, where she was willing to give up her desire to follow a particular career path, in the hope that it would speed up the process of matrimony with him.

Though C actively chose H and K as intimate relationships, intimacy in itself was a difficult terrain for her to traverse. Intimate gestures would collapse into abuse for her and she would find herself accusing both H and K, in different ways, of violation. In both these cases, there seemed to be the same pattern—a moment of intimacy that rekindled a sense of trauma, a reaction, and accusation at her end, which involved bringing it to the notice of the boy's family and partially her own. This was followed by a resolution that either involved her giving up the relationship (in H's case), or giving up a part of herself that, until now, she identified with (in K's case). C seemed to unconsciously repeat her initial trauma, where she was in a passive position, in an attempt to occupy a more active role in it. In the process of this, she also attempted to reconcile with a part that wanted to belong to the community in some way or the other, if not as the liberal thinking woman, then as the good dutiful Muslim who married within the community. Though there remained an awareness in C's mind of these positions, this compulsion to repeat seemed to have a unconscious hold over her beyond her conscious control. Here, it seemed the pleasure principle no longer retained dominion, and it was only through an experience of unpleasure that some pleasure in intimacy and a feeling of belongingness could be retained. Consequently, no matter what she thought about the relationship internally, at the level of community, despite their history, the decision to marry K was only contested to some extent by her mother and her aunt. The rest of the family felt that she chose a potential suitor at the appropriate marriageable age. The choice was clear, no matter the cost.

Reflections on the Analytic Association

What struck me most about C was her need to have an external order in response to an internal chaos. The expression in the referral form was telling, not just of her presenting complaints, but the way she navigated them for herself. Oscillating between a sense of urgency and absence, she felt a strong need to absent herself from the situation, when urgency was experienced and communicated. This dynamic became most apparent in her missing of or absence from sessions. Due to the collapse of trauma and controversy, I wondered whether at times, therapy became a place for confession. If it did, how difficult was it to return to that space. This became most apparent in the way she introduced gaps in the sessions. Though the gaps seemed arbitrary to her, to me it communicated a relationship with interruption. I felt that if we sustained an internal focus on her too long, something in her would come unhinged, and she could not afford that. I wondered what therapy became for her in these moments and as an extension, who I became.

Two women, of similar age and life stage, talked to each other. At the same time, two communities talked to each other. The fear of being judged always loomed in the room, as did the memory of interrupted conversations. Yet, the response she received in this space seemed to be a response she hadn't seen before. She carried it outside the room in a different way, as a renewed trust in relationships with other women who had, at some point, been friends and allies. Though it's difficult to say this with certainty, as our work together began to take form, she allowed others in her life some access to herself, to her struggles, and to her strengths. She found herself rekindling old friendships and talking about where she was internally, at moments stating her vulnerability, at other moments helping a friend through theirs. Basic trust seemed to be returning, allowing her to find a voice once more.

There were many instances where I identified with her struggle of charting a career trajectory for herself while maintaining a balance in her relationships. That pressure didn't feel alien nor did her response to it. As she struggled to bring together her liberal thinking self with the self that was struggling to find a middle ground closer to home, I experienced myself as an ally, which in itself was confusing. Despite moments of collaboration, we were different. And the difference was most stark in the religious identities we occupied. Her stating that difference made me acknowledge it for myself in a very different way, and that was important in our work.

Many injunctions had been made on C's sense of self and these labels had impacted her deeply. Though it was important to connect with those struggles, it was equally important to know that the impact of some of them would not reach me and I could only have access to them through their impact on her. Perhaps this made therapy a controversial space—the fact that the most unspeakable things were being talked about and engaged with.

Towards the end of our work together the first time around, she became more aware of me, not just as different from her but as a separate person. On one such occasion, she noticed the ink pen I was using to write her receipt: 'It's so enticing, the way you write with an ink pen … you make it look so effortless.' I believe she wasn't just talking about the pen but the multiple things we were navigating within the session and outside it as individuals too. In our last session together, she had touched upon an experience of awkwardness— 'I feel I have become attached to you' —and wondered whether she had the option of coming back to therapy at a later time, when she felt better placed to explore more. I had left that option open, depending on how both of us were placed at the time. As we parted ways, she gave me a wrapped-up book. She picked up on my hesitance but insisted it wasn't anything big, just a small thank you. I only looked at it once she left. As I walked her out, she paused at the door for a moment and said, 'So … See you, but I guess not see you? Soon.' She took a deep breath and left. My sense was that she wouldn't hesitate to return if she needed to, and that to me, felt like the strength of our work, that a space had been opened up for her, which she could return to. As I came back to the room and looked at the diary, it had a bright vibrant cover with a lot of colours and a peacock drawn on it, with a note inside that said, 'Thank you for your support and help.'

I carried a sense as though something had moved, and something had been contained, for the moment, and had found symbolization in the diary, something vibrant and colourful, with a sturdy texture, a possibility of writing something for herself too, as though a process of formation was beginning, and C had found a medium to explore that in.

As our work came to a final close, after her return, the texture of that final session was a bit different from this one. In the short second chapter of our work, it seemed that C had made up her mind; there was no confusion regarding whether she should go through with the relationship with K or not. With all that had happened, where she too had been actively involved, the only way she would be able to live with this henceforth, would be to remain in it, no matter what that did to her. Though my concerns were always closer to what kind of relationship she would have with K, given all that had happened, C remained close to a sense of what is right, what needs to be done, and what a good Muslim girl should do. For whatever the struggles between C and K were, they were between them; she was no longer in opposition to her family, her community, or her larger social understanding of a woman of age 26. In ending work, the subject position she cast me in was one of outside the community, too liberal in thought, bringing in things she did not want to think about. Possibly this projection, and subsequently the cessation of our work, also allowed her to return to her sense of community.

In her work with me, C allied with the woman subject, where trauma and an experience of violation could be talked about, despite its controversial nature. At moments, she would use me as an ally, a sounding board who she could think about these moments with, in the hope that I would understand them and not question their truth and validity. In contrast to this, as she struggled with her identity of being Muslim, she carried the sense that I, as a Hindu, couldn't possibly understand the experience of being Muslim in our present context. She carried what she described as a 'sense of paranoia' about being misunderstood or being misused, owing to her social location. At the point that our work came to end, she marked a distance between these two identity elements, her sense being: 'I don't want to be reminded about this anymore and I need to do what needs to be done.' In this moment, I felt she constructed me as a particular repository of those parts that she had to leave behind, in an attempt to go ahead with her decision to marry K. This moment, for me, carried a representational sense of suicidality that did not present itself through the act of harming oneself, but instead presented a tussle between parts of the self; where the killing of one could precipitate the survival of the other.

X's Case

X has been one of the most challenging patients I have worked with, while also being close to the preoccupations with suicidality that this work is attempting to theorize. From the beginning of the work, to its end, X remained consistently preoccupied with the desire to end his life, a preoccupation that had resulted in attempts at the same, prior to our beginning work together. Over the 14 months of our work, it remained important to me to be a reliable presence for X, as much as possible. X had a timeline he wanted to follow, a deadline by which he would not only terminate therapy, but also his life. He would sometimes use this timeline to try to undermine any attempt at reflection, a deflection from any exploration of his life history or internal world, while also creating a constant sense of pressure around the likelihood of an attempt. At other moments, X would seem like a lost younger self, unable to find a way to be in the world. The world around him seemed violent and daunting, and his sense of himself remained one of being lacking—emotionally, physically, intellectually—unable to go on, not having the right mechanisms to get too far in life. As a result, in his progression of thoughts, death was the only solution that could rid him of this feeling of 'stuckness', this sense of depression, and this deep sense of inadequacy.

While for the initial part of our work, I remained most concerned with X's preoccupation with ending his life, his desire for death, and the images he evoked around it, I soon began to wonder, who would X be if he wasn't someone who wanted to take his life in March 2018? As I became more acquainted with the parts in him that felt dead or close to death, I wondered about parts that could provide vitality, whether something in his milieu lent to an alive sense of self? In this tussle, between being and not being, did something get interrupted in X's striving towards identity formation?

In my work with X, I encountered the difficulty and challenges posed by a sustained engagement with suicidality, not just within the subject, but also in interaction with the subject. X occupied my mind space in a way that other subjects did not and though that was important, I wonder what it did to the nature of my work with him and others within the clinic.

Waiting to Begin: The Initial Encounter

X had waited to begin therapy and was assigned to me due to his preoccupations with suicide. Though his reasons for referral were stated in one word— 'depression', a consultation note written in November 2016 by a colleague informed me that X was intending to take his life in 2018. This made me curious about X and I wondered about his relationship to death. What would it mean to decide a time to end life much in advance, and having done so, what were his expectations of therapy? X was 24 years old when we began working together in April 2017. I was hesitant to begin work with him as I was aware of an upcoming internship that I would be required to do, for which I may have needed to travel. Simultaneously, there was an awareness that X had been waiting too long, so a few consultations were set up to access where he was at.

X had a long history of depression beginning in 2010, which got aggravated after his Class 12 results. He first attempted to take his life at this point, by jumping off the second floor. Subsequently, he had attempted three other times: by trying to hang himself from a fan, by suffocating himself, and by ingesting poison. He had been on medication for depression which started after his first attempt. Since 2015, he has also been medicated for OCD, diagnosed because of his obsession with taking his life. He had begun therapy at that time: a few sessions, which he found rather unhelpful. He moved to another therapist and worked with her for a few months. Though he found it helpful this time and felt quite fond of her, he eventually ended therapy because of 'erotic transference issues'. He then decided to start psychoanalytic psychotherapy, which became too expensive to sustain as he was unemployed. When I began work with him, he had started a new job at a risk analysis firm.

X had a lot of questions about the clinic, the fee, whether that was an incentive to my working, whether I was a trainee, and what my specialization was if I had any. He also enquired as to whether the sessions were recorded in any manner. He seemed mistrustful and fairly certain from the onset that I would not be able to take on his case. Despite that sense, in the next three meetings, he gave me a detailed narration of his history, after cross checking whether I had access to it already.

X did not seem comfortable talking about his family and in an attempt to negotiate that he provided minimal information. His brother, who was seven years older than him, was diagnosed with schizo-affective disorder when X was quite young. He recalled his brother as someone who was both violent and hyperactive. X would constantly find himself in the middle of fights between his brother and his parents. His parents found it difficult to deal with his brother and in an attempt to not let things escalate between them, X would get involved. There was always a lot of violence in the house, but he did not seem to have access to that as he narrated it.

He described himself as someone who had 'adjustment issues' and found it difficult to interact with people. He remembered having suicidal thoughts as early as 2007, when he was in Class 9. In his understanding, low mood and social anxiety had been constant contributing factors to the same. He planned his first attempt soon after his class 12 results came out, as he was unable to get into medical school. He went to Shimla and jumped off the second floor of the hotel he was staying in. He survived with just a fractured leg. X's parents were informed and initially they thought he had been kidnapped and that the call was made to create panic. When they realized that the case was different, they did not seem to have much of a reaction. He said they were concerned 'but what else could they do, really'.

While describing his 'triggers' X said in one breath,

I was not doing as well as I would have liked to in my life.

And my brother was also being violent.

Things were not good at home.

In 2007/2008 I had some good friends who helped. There were people that I could talk to.

When I joined school, I designed a project, but by the end of it I didn't have the energy to sustain it. I couldn't keep up with trying to be friends with people.

I joined coaching classes for engineering exams but that dampened my self-esteem.

I didn't have the mental strength to do those exams. I couldn't mug everything up. I did that in college and I graduated on purpose.

I had a six-month gap between college and my first job.

Between June and December 2014. I tried to hang myself 2–3 times.

When I joined work, it was a rather challenging environment. I couldn't continue.

I had suicidal thoughts throughout this time.

The first time I went in for therapy, it was in 2015 on and off.

In August close to my birthday I resigned. This was the time when my brother was deteriorating. He needed to be hospitalized against his will.

In 2013 my grandfather died, I was close to him.

Soon after that my grandmother who used to live with us also died.

Then my uncle died.

My pet also died.

As I heard him talk about the many things that had impacted him, I felt a deep sense of sadness. The consultations felt overwhelming and information heavy: intended for me to create a timeline of what his life had been. Yet, I felt that I didn't know much about him. I did not have a grip on the affective rhythms in his life. The sense of depression felt deep and it also felt difficult to move past that. This became a continuous theme in our work together. On the one hand, it would feel like X was flooding the room with detailed chronological information; on the other, it felt like X was withholding information and refusing to go in any other direction but the ones that he had chosen. In between what was being said, and what wasn't being brought to dialogue, I wondered how therapy could help X, and more importantly whether he wanted that help.

The Search for a Confirmation: Diagnosis as Deflection

From the beginning of the work itself, X began to press for a diagnosis. My hesitance to go into one so early on in our work made him question my training. He was aware of the fact that I was a trainee and would use that awareness to dismiss anything I had to offer. He believed that I hadn't had a chance to consult my supervisors and that I should do so immediately so that he can get his answers. He didn't feel open to an exploration around this fantasy. He used diagnosis as a tool to understand himself and continue work on that, outside therapy. I believe that he carried an idea of a diagnosis of himself and he just wanted a confirmation of the same. The confirmation would further validate his plan and his decision. It felt like he was pushing me to confirm his life was indeed not worth living.

Any attempt at an exploration of life themes, affects, or states of mind was interrupted, or shut down. He used a lot of technical jargon while talking about himself, almost in a self-explanatory manner. Terms like transference, acting out, feelings of abandonment, splitting, intellectualization as a defence were a part of his vocabulary but it was difficult to surmise what they meant to him. He found exploration of any kind irrelevant to what he needed and felt that these would only be deviations from the plan he had in mind. 'I have spent a lot of time building up my arguments, like a monument. And I don't want to alter or change anything in that monument. I've spent a lot of time building it.' If I tried to push him a little further to think about it all, he would threaten to terminate work. The deadline of March 2018 was communicated to me at the beginning of our work together. He felt that this timeline would be conducive since his father would be retiring then and there would be a monetary inflow because of that. X didn't feel ready to explore this decision, but wanted to devise ways to prevent and control grief. He felt fairly certain that his family would be least impacted if this timeline was deployed. In case there was any impact, he wanted to create mechanisms to deal with that for them. It seemed like X didn't want to explore why he thought this was the only way or how he had got here, but now that he had, he wanted help in taking what he felt were the 'necessary steps forward'. He would say, in a matter-of-fact manner, that his 'natural state (was) that suicide is the best option' and he 'didn't intend on staying here very long'. As I heard him say these things, I felt like X did not have a choice about finding himself in this state and I wondered how it had come to that. It felt like X had resigned himself to this state and as I heard him say these things, I wondered how he had got here. I began to experience my own curiosities as violent, because anything I asked or sought to clarify would evoke rage in X. He would shut me down by saying 'How do you not know this?', 'How unprofessional of you' or 'You really need to think about whether you want to be in this profession!' Initially, it was difficult to get past my own sense of inadequacy while working with X, since these statements came close to what I was grappling with internally as a trainee.

Throughout the work, X seemed preoccupied with his desire to end his life on the one hand, and the process of therapy on the other. In contradiction to his certainty about leaving therapy soon, X also expressed a desire to increase the frequency and intensity of therapy. These curiosities surfaced gradually, with a backdrop of an image of a child part that also entered the room with the adult part, who is rather aware that he isn't equipped to make it through life. This split was something that he was aware of and his purpose in therapy, as he understood it, was to entertain the child in him that he brought with himself, and eventually allow the latter to be led by the adult, who had decided on the course of action: death. I wondered whether this was a split between the child and the adult, or two children fighting for a certain kind of attention. X would, in a derogatory tone, dismiss his preoccupations saying: 'maybe I am doing all this for attention'. As I tried to think with him about what needed attending to, X would find it difficult to explore this need and would state that this was definitely a bad thing and there was nothing more to explore there.

On the Nature of Suicidality: Death and its Images

X would bring with him multiple images of death. He was looking for a 'painless way to die', as mentioned before. He did extensive research on the possible methods but he did not want to discuss his choices with me as he was worried that I would inform someone else. As I asked him more about his unsuccessful attempt post school, he talked about how difficult it was to have survived that: 'It's like I can't even get this right.' According to him, his parents did not have much of a response to his first attempt, but the people who discovered him beat him and kicked him for attempting to take his life. Though he was surprised he had landed on his feet, the sight of blood had scared him. He couldn't understand why they were calling him names but was thankful they had not called the police. At the same time, he felt a sense of humiliation at failing at dying, more than attempting. He had threatened to crash the car when he was driving back with his father and they were arguing about his preoccupation with death. His father had had no response. On one occasion, X had felt that shooting himself would be the best option because it would be quick; however the worry was that it could be painful. In a session in the later part of our work, while looking at a wire that connected the AC in the room he exclaimed, 'I love the wire there, I never had a long enough wire when I was attempting. This one seems long enough.' The rope that he had used to hang himself in a previous attempt had broken, resulting in another comic failure. Though I don't think he experienced it as funny. At other junctures, he thought about euthanasia and the concoction that is used for the same. He felt it would be fair for him to be euthanized, because his life till now had proven to him that he wouldn't be able to make it through. These statements were stated like facts; questions or exploration around these assumptions were experienced as intolerable and he would actively shut them down.

Yet, at moments, almost despite himself, something would ease and allow him to freely associate. One such association occurred as he talked about his pet. I was struck by the impersonal way in which he talked about his pet, who later came in as an important companion and was one of the few characters in X's life that carried a dimension which he was ready to bring into the room. He recalled, 'I would notice that he would bite himself really hard, till he bled sometimes, I think he used to do that to feel something.' There was something important to X about this association but he didn't go into it immediately. A few sessions later, he talked about how he had been instrumental in putting his dog to sleep. As he was the only one who took care of him, he realized that he was suffering too much and should be put out of his misery. He felt similarly about himself and wondered why being put out of his misery was not an available option.

Between Working Together and Working Alone: The Nature of the Dyad

X felt that he wasn't winning at 'this game of life', and that he had actively withdrawn from his family in 2005. He found it difficult to interact with people and kept to himself. He kept his interactions at work to a minimum, and his only other social interaction seemed to be with his therapists. He felt it important to see female therapists and his sense was that this was coming from his 'need to have a female anchor in his life'. X spent a lot of time thinking about therapy and what to say in each session. He maintained a diary of his thoughts and associations, an excel sheet on the number of minutes he was given in each session, and a list of pros and cons of being in therapy. He wouldn't share this in the session, but felt it important to point out moments when he felt he wasn't being given enough time. As the work continued, moments of spontaneous interaction began to increase. X would catch himself at these moments and, occasionally, interrupt his own thoughts. At other times, he would smile at being able to feel something in the moment and think about it, even though he wasn't always able to say it out loud. He felt that the child part seemed to look forward to seeing me but the adult part was concerned that it might feel a 'tug'.

He was late for our 16th session. One could see how absolutely intolerable this was for him. Since it had also been raining that day, I assumed that there must have been traffic, but to him that was 'just an excuse'. The fact that I was being perfectly understanding about it only made him feel more frustrated. He said then that therapy was a waste of his time, not just his time, but my time too. Someone else could benefit more from this space, since despite wanting to use it, he did not know how to. Though he had talked about termination before for other reasons, in this session the desire to leave therapy seemed to be coming from having kept me waiting. It was difficult for him to talk about this and think it through, so in the next few sessions he wondered whether some psychological testing could be done on him, maybe a Rorschach.

As we discussed this further, X felt the need for a test because 'it will help with my diagnosis and allow me to work on myself on my own'. The idea of working together seemed to be difficult to grasp for him. Yet, in all this communication, there seemed to be a deep desire to be known without communicating. My sense was that X was equally confused about my stance in therapy. Though he had a sense of the process of therapy, he didn't feel open to exploration; yet it was clear that he wanted help and at moments also needed it. This is precisely what the 'tug' was.

In the absence of giving in to the need for a diagnosis, X began to go into long silences in the sessions. These moments of silence did not feel constrictive or defensive. I asked him where his mind goes when he is silent and he said, 'I know termination is nearby, and when I say anything, you take me down a rabbit hole and I don't want to go there now. There is no point.' Contrary to the nature of our conversation, which was largely combative, in silence, X seemed to be more in touch with how he was feeling about my presence. This was an important movement in our work together: in becoming aware of what my presence was doing to him, X was allowing himself to work with me, as opposed to working on his own.

X: I haven't been able to resolve erotic transference.
   I heard someone ask you where your bag was before the session.
Me: How did that make you feel?
X: I thought you had forgotten about the session.
   But you're consistent.
   You were here on time

He had seen me interacting with colleagues in the corridor prior to our session. Though this evoked some feelings in him, it's difficult to know how he felt. He clubbed it under the term 'erotic transference'.

There seemed to be a longing to be intimately involved, but that felt pre-adolescent, where the distance between the self and the other is not sharply marked. I wondered if he used terms such as 'erotic transference' in order to distance himself from the affect he felt. It seemed to me that he *felt* deeply, and that was a threatening experience for him.

Playing Dead/Terminating/Termination

Death seemed to be a way of integration for X, or at least the easiest way to be coherent. As we attempted to explore what else could be a moment of integration, there was a deep sense of sadness in the room. X expressed the desire to go to a 'death therapist', who could help him wrap up his affairs before he left in March. At the same time, he wanted to minimize the impact his death might have on others. For the adult in him, things were quantitative and feelings irrelevant. Gradually, a sense of curiosity with regard to the latter had begun to emerge.

X felt that he had begun enacting his plan of taking his life by increasingly going silent in the sessions: by 'playing dead'. He felt that the tussle between the child and the adult, and the exhaustion it brought, could only be salvaged in death. That would be the only relief. We tried to think of alternative ways of integrating these two parts. The child part seemed preservative to his psychic makeup; it was clearly a healthy part. This was the part that brought him to therapy, made him seek help, and continue work. It made an appearance in the sessions when he associated more freely, and when he wasn't preoccupied with termination, erotic transference, and diagnosis. It smiles, I brought that to his awareness. On an otherwise grim face, there would be an occasional smile. He agreed. He found the child part arrogant, and it is that arrogance that resulted in him being pushed to a corner. I wondered if the adult part was scared, and as I said this to him, the smile disappeared. He looked thoughtful, and asked me why I thought that. I said, 'I wonder, when an adult part of us steps in to protect the child part, almost prematurely, could it be premised on fear?' I was thinking about him as that child, with a violent brother, who had to step in to protect his parents. I thought about the fear in that moment, when things were so out of control, and a young self, developing around the need to control, to calculate, to create an excel sheet. He was silent when I said this and he nodded, 'you're right'. In the past, any attempt to integrate my thoughts, and give them to him had been met with a certain degree of attack. He usually wouldn't let me complete the thought, or would shut it down, or dismiss it. He had done none of it this time. As the session ended, I felt gifted by an openness that, I felt, could be helpful in our work.

X's preoccupation with taking his life seemed to present itself in more than one way. It would make its appearance felt in planning for the event, and creating a sound argument for his decision, despite his ambivalence around the same. His suicidality seemed to be located in his ambivalence around mutuality. My attempts to engage with his thoughts and feelings also established me as separate from him; a separation that, at moments, felt intolerable. His attempts to think through this, by himself, enhanced the feelings of isolation and loneliness. Yet, this silence allowed for something more undifferentiated, possibly also a space to recover something from within himself, which would then allow him to communicate to me (and at moments even to himself) as someone separate. This tussle became more apparent in moments of enactment, which seemed to bring spontaneity and symbolization simultaneously.

X's decision, that life was not worth living, seemed to have a quality of pre-matureness. This quality presented itself in sessions as well. In saying that he couldn't be helped, and that all the data he had gathered proved that he couldn't make it through life, X seemed to be creating a situation where helping him would be impossible, even as he was actively seeking help. Perhaps this was his attempt at communicating how deeply he needed help to return to a sense of life with meaning. X seemed to have a degree of awareness that he was withholding information to retain control in an otherwise chaotic life; I wondered what picture he would paint, if only he was able to.

Open at the Close: Attempted Moments of Meeting

In our 22nd session, post-Diwali, X got me a card that didn't open. Two pieces of paper stuck together with the line *Thank You Ambika*, with my name highlighted in yellow. He had felt grateful for the work we had been doing, and for the fact that I hadn't cancelled the session, despite it being the day after a national holiday. As soon as he expressed this, he felt the need to take it back, tear it to pieces, and burn it. I felt the need to put my hand gently on the card, as he continued to talk about how he wanted to destroy it. Through the card, I felt that X was beginning to symbolize something for himself, and communicate it to me. Two sessions later, X made a disclosure, 'My grandmother had told me this story, that my mother had tried to take her life before I was born. Apparently, she had a miscarriage. I don't entirely believe her, but I haven't asked… I don't want to.' He refused to explore it further; this session was the first time that his mother had made an appearance. There was something in X that now began to look anticipatory, which brought to mind the image of a traffic light; like the yellow in the card, X was somewhere between the red of stopping, and the green of moving forward.

It was difficult to say what had moved in X, but in the sessions that followed, he brought up termination in December 2017 as a definitive possibility. His sense was that he wanted to terminate because he had come to care for me, and didn't want me to be affected by his life choices; he simultaneously maintained that there was no way that I could be affected, since I was a therapist. As we talked about loss and mourning, I tried to think with him about this gesture, and how it contained within it a wish: a desire to impact the other person. He refuted that by saying that, 'one moves on, and if anyone, you have the resources to do it!' As we explored this further, I tried to open up his imagination of mourning, and how one moves through it, but 'doesn't really get over it'. To illustrate this, I mentioned his difficulty in talking about the loss of his dog, even though it had been a considerable length of time since. He smiled at this and said, 'There is a part that is happy to see you and glad that you're here.' Yet the tussle continued, between needing me to be impacted by him and his gestures, and retracting every time I was.

He talked about what it was like for him when his brother got diagnosed. He was very young at the time, and felt responsible for what was happening to all of them. His father had a breakdown, and suffered a heart attack. He blamed his mother, and though the mother tried to handle the situation, at moments she just couldn't. Soon after, she started practising meditation, to put something at ease for herself. X was sent to stay at his uncle's house at this point, so that he could be taken care of. He felt safe there, but he found it difficult to stay away from his parents, as he feared for their safety. X's brother was more overtly violent by this time, and even now, X worried that his brother could badly injure his parents. X seemed to have grown up in an environment with a lot of violence. As he grew older, he became better at handling his brother. Still, his sense of fear was palpable when he talked about it. X felt mistrustful and unsafe in most environments, including therapy. Though he began to talk about his family, my sense was that X felt the need to destabilize me by going back to his preoccupation with death. Perhaps, a desire to take his life also allowed for a degree of control over something which had felt beyond one's control. The idea of death as a hopeful escape, or a controlled response to a difficult life, came to mind, and I hoped we would be able to explore this further. Perhaps if we could move past the desire to terminate. Perhaps termination was a similar kind of repetition as well.

As X began to open up more, he felt uncertain about coming for therapy. He felt the need to constantly remind me of his deadline, and that he was looking for 'the right kind of nudge for March 2018'. He didn't want to explore this deadline any further than that, or what he had in mind regarding the same. He established this in each session: that he was going to do it, and not talk about it. My sense is, that it also helped him talk about other things in his life, which felt equally difficult. X felt responsible for his brother's breakdown, and felt that he should have been more aware of it as a child. He felt angry with himself for not being better at managing him. He recalled having locked himself in his grandparents' house for five days straight, after his brother's diagnosis had been confirmed. He felt he was trying to transform into someone who could deal with that by isolating himself. 'Isolation allows me to put pressure to transform.' As he said this,

I had the image of putting something very large in a very small box. I also became more aware of the room.

As he talked about how he should have had a better handle on things, we tried to further open up his expectations of himself as the youngest member of the family. He responded to this by talking about the cost of being in therapy, and how someone else would benefit so much more. It was as if he believed that the need of the other is more than his own, in content and intensity; the wish remained that his need be given space, more than it required. X's struggle with how he 'would have liked to be', and how he 'was', became more apparent. Much had contributed to who he was today, a lot of which was beyond his control. It was difficult for X to access that, and in that moment, I felt deeply sad for him. He wasn't always this person, and a lot of who he had become seemed to be the only way he could have preserved something for himself, and his loved ones. X wondered if he was 'well adjusted' or 'maladaptive' in the way he thought of life. He once recalled, 'There was a tube light in my room. It stopped working. It would bother me, but I didn't say anything about it. One day, after many years, my father came in and changed it.' He smiled as he said this. There was clearly a part that hoped things would change, and there would be light, but it was too scary to ask for that, especially to be refused that. Here care was experienced in action, rather than in words. He felt grateful for the simple gesture of the tube light being changed.

Passing the Dead/line: A Continuation...

As we crossed his self-imposed deadline for termination in December, X talked about wanting to move closer to death, and his anxieties around that. He had started talking to his parents about his desire to die. His mother was worried that 'the negative thoughts had returned' and wanted him to meditate as a line of defence. He felt that she didn't get it, and recounted how they had had to put his dog to sleep because there was no hope for him. He felt that his situation was similar. As we tried to explore what evoked this sense of similarity, the loop in the conversation began once more. He talked about his sense of professional failure and not making it very far in life, as though it was independent of what was happening in his life at the time. Though he could see the link I was trying to make, he found it difficult to believe it, and felt that he was using it as an excuse. Simultaneously, he also felt that I was trying to engage with him, and he felt the need to 'award' me for that. He handed me a box that read *best T – 2017*, similar in form to the card he had given me earlier. It contained a mug that would show the constellations when hot water was put into it. He said,

> I wonder if they award you for the work you do, I just think you should be, it doesn't seem very easy. I think this is pretty much the last thing I'd give you, or maybe a card when we end work before March, but now we seem to be continuing.

I had heard reward instead of award. I wondered about this gesture, and his need to give me something. What felt relieving, in this moment, was the agreement to continue work.

As the sessions progressed from January 2018 onwards, X began to bring more concrete preoccupations: *how do I deal with loss? Why have my attempts been non–lethal? Am I emotionally stunted? I think I'm borderline but I don't meet the entire criteria… how does one work with that?* These questions were stated plainly, and sometimes, it felt like he was doing it to retain my curiosity. Exploring these questions was difficult, because of the air of pointlessness everything carried for X. There was a profound sense of emptiness and despair, which was accessible in the room, but it was difficult for me to get a sense of what the problem was. It seemed self-explanatory to him, and yet when we tried to explore it, we seemed to be stuck in a loop. It began to feel more and more like taking his life was a permanent solution to a temporary problem, a problem that was too difficult to talk about, maybe because he also could not articulate what it was. I wondered who he would be if he wasn't preoccupied with life and death; would he be able to hold a conversation or be retained in the mind if he wasn't presenting a crisis? His own experience had been of compliance and non-reactivity when his brother was in crisis. Did he believe that the brother received more attention and now he needed attending to? I wondered whether he would make an attempt in March; would he alternate between feeling fairly certain he wouldn't, and cautious about the fact that he might. A part of me also felt he might end therapy, just to leave that question lingering.

Throughout March, X seemed to be withdrawing and becoming more combative in our interactions. He firmly pressed for a 'formulation', as opposed to a diagnosis, bringing in a language he thought I would be more comfortable with. Though these moments in the past had made me feel pushed to a corner and inadequate, this time around, I felt more certain that I did not have access to enough information to say much more. I brought this to his awareness, that despite transacting in data and choosing what he would like to engage with in therapy, he hadn't really explored his emotional landscape with me. He seemed proud of this, but it was also what felt most counterproductive to the work. He wanted to be in charge of his care, or wanted me to take an unambiguous stance that I cared. This polarity made it difficult for a flow in the work to be established. He opened up one session with a desire to explore and combated any attempt to open anything up. Then what were we doing in this space? He felt that in his 'clinical judgement', my biggest error in this work had been 'not increasing the frequency'. This seemed to be a new variant of a dynamic that had played out in our work before. Initially, it came as refusal to go in any direction, and then refusal came through the avenue of his clinical opinion. We reached a juncture where he could not tolerate me saying anything in the session, and my silence also became unhinging to him. I seemed to be a carrying a sense of attack and I wondered about how close that was to his experience.

As we explored what the end of March meant for him, he oscillated between the conviction that he wasn't going to take his life, and feeling infuriated at not being prepared enough. The question of what his expectation of therapy was, became important to reopen. It had become clear to him that therapy was pro-life, and wasn't going to help him kill himself in the way that he wanted; yet he continued to come. His explanation was that he had given a lot of time to therapy, and there is some truth to that. However, in the time I had worked with him, he had remained constricted and withholding, which was akin to how he seemed to have experienced me. X seemed to be communicating from a regressed state, while attempting to maintain the façade of coherent structure. Controlling what information was given seemed to be an attempt to control my mind, and the way it responded, while hoping that it could intuit his needs. It was difficult not to take his relationship with suicidality seriously, considering the four attempts, and yet there seemed to be so much more that he was not bringing into the sessions. Especially his emotional and relational dynamics. Any moment of separation or mutuality was difficult to access or tolerate. If the act of suicide establishes a clear separation from the other, while the communication around suicidality requires an other, X found himself torn between these two positions, constantly struggling between being, or not being.

Reflections on the Analytic Association

In working with X, I felt a deep pull of sadness. A sadness so profound, that at moments it would represent itself as X's defiance of the therapeutic structure. It would present itself in a sense of mistrust of my own motivations for being present to his struggles. X constantly posed questions about the structure of therapy, in a manner that would, at times, make me feel pushed and anxious. At other times, I would wonder what X was trying to process and create for himself, amid this tussle. As I felt the need to create a sense of consistency, X responded to it by always being there for the session; he never missed any session without prior notice, and was hardly ever late. Any disruption of this consistency would feel intolerable to X, and that felt like a communication of the kind of environment he felt he needed in order to be able to survive.

X took a long time to talk about his family and his home environment. My sense was that something about it remained too painful, unprocessed, and unsymbolized. He felt responsible for his brother's illness, and for what his brother could and did further inflict on his parents. His parents seemed to be experienced as passive entities, unable to manage the brother, unable to take care of themselves or X. There was some respite with the grandparents; their death possibly interrupted something more for X, making it difficult for him to be anything more than the position that he had come to occupy—as someone who would be unable to make it through life—where death becomes the only solution.

More than helplessness at X's plight, there was always a deeper sense of sadness. At moments, it felt like his preoccupation with death, talking about it, thinking about it, allowed him the space to not attempt it. But precisely this thought also felt most dangerous, because he had attempted to take his life before, so what would prevent him from doing so now? As we continued to work together, I felt I was constantly being tested, if I passed the test, X would defer his impulse; but if I didn't, I wondered what X was capable of doing. I felt it important to draw X's awareness to the parts of him that continued to avow life, without losing cognizance of those parts that were preoccupied with death. Just like how the adult parts were not without the child parts. But X experienced himself as constantly split, at moments painfully so, and it remained difficult for him to move in a direction that allowed him to think about that.

It was difficult to get a sense of who X was. His version of himself was of someone barely managing, deeply lacking, unable to be present to anything or anyone. However, throughout the time we worked together, X was employed, present for family trips and interactions, and regular in attending his sessions with me. It was clear that he didn't like being a part of the first two, but despite that, he would manage to participate. His internal standard of what would be a good enough position to achieve in life not only prevented him from going further, but also made him undermine everything he had achieved.

X's history is not an easy one. To live with a family member with mental illness, and on most occasions be the primary caregiver to them, had taken an exacting toll on his understanding of himself. It felt like in the absence of having any positive markers for the development of his identity, he had picked up negative aspects of those around him. In response to me, sometimes he occupied what he called the child-like part, while at others, he seemed to be responding from a part that felt more explorative of his own sexuality. Sexuality, as a theme, could not be explored beyond the term 'erotic transference'; it seemed too threatening for X to think about further. I couldn't find the right language to explore it myself, and carried his hesitation with me.

X's suicidality sought many symbolic forms in our work together. It would present itself in moments where he would talk about his desire to terminate therapy almost synonymously with terminating his life, which remained a constant tussle in the work. Parallel to this, was a desire to be received and remembered. It was difficult for him to recognize his feelings, but what remained even more difficult for him to experience, was recognition in itself. His desire to take back and tear the card that he had given me, and my need to not allow that, was perhaps not anticipated by him. This element of surprise allowed him to experience something different from his expectation. Reception, instead of rejection. In my work with him, I felt it important to receive these gestures and return to them, with him, in an attempt to process what was being symbolized through them.

My work with X ended in June 2018, much after his termination of therapy deadline, also beyond his deadline of March 2018. Our last two months of work were especially difficult as X began to close up, and felt miserable about not being able 'even [to] do this right!' He assumed an opposite position within this time, stating that he had actually never been suicidal and hadn't intended to take his life in March anyway. This switch confused me and made me feel intensely angry. I think it was in these moments that I felt closest to the madness he grapples with—between being and not being, fact and fantasy— who was he? It remains a question that stays with us.

In our last session, X read out a written piece, which he wanted me to patiently listen to before beginning the process of termination. He went over our entire work together, moments where he had lost his temper, moments where I had lost mine, the themes we had gone through, moments he felt like I hadn't understood what he was saying, and moments in which he felt he had crossed the line. He felt both apologetic, and grateful for the space he had had. I began to feel that he had been more present to this process than it had seemed like, at times.

At the end of this session, A handed me another card. It was similar to the first one. A large thank you in front, two pages stuck together that didn't open. But this time, the back of the card had a small drawing of a penguin. The penguin looks like it is waving and though I smiled seeing that, a deep sense of sadness returned. It wasn't anxiety about what X might do to himself, whether he would make another attempt or not; it felt like some of our work had retained itself with X, enough for the child part to communicate once more. Along with this, X also handed me two legal documents, since I hadn't instituted a formal no suicide contract. I think he found it outlandish of me, but it seemed like this also facilitated the work, while adding a deep strain as well. I wished I hadn't taken the contract from him, but in hindsight, I wonder if this exchange was also an exchange of care and mutual recognition, of a termination of therapy, but not the termination of the will to live?

In X's case, the nature and contours of suicidality became a sustained preoccupation, occupying a position between failed attempts at suicide and the desire for a final successful attempt. The desire to die, bringing an end to everything, appeared as an active preoccupation in X's narrative. In contrast to this, X often occupied a passive position in response to his brother's violent episodes. X's brother had a long history of mental illness which had deeply impacted X in ways that were difficult for him to articulate. He experienced his brother as overly active, sometimes hyper, and as having a propensity for deep violence. X, on the other hand, would feel small in these moments, concerned and anxious for his brother, but more so for the kind of violence he was capable of unleashing on both X and his parents. His brother came across as an unstoppable force, while X's parents would occupy a degree of passivity, both in dealing with his brother and in intervening with him, when things got out of hand. X's mother would retreat into herself and turned towards meditation in an attempt to contain the matter for herself, while X's father would actively blame his wife for the way both the boys turned out. Active and passive positions played themselves out within the family where X's brother and father occupied an active overt stance, often resulting in a retreat into passivity for X and his mother. At other moments, X's parents would retreat from his brother's active violence, often making X the custodian of his brother. Though X deeply cared for his brother, he carried a deep sense of violation and rage which was too difficult to bear. He couldn't very easily unleash it on his brother, so he contained it within himself. My sense is, this uncontained rage found expression in his attempts at taking his life and his interactions with his therapists.

X had been in and out of therapy for a long time before we began our work together. Though he carried a sense that therapy could be useful to him, he also maintained that he was beyond help. He often occupied a position of expertise, devaluing the therapist, making it clear that they were unable to do their job adequately. He carried this impression of his previous therapists and re-enacted this in our interaction as well. At moments, I would feel deeply struck by X's remarks and it felt to me as though he was attacking a part of me that already felt shaky. It took some time before I could bring this back to him as something to think about. X had a deep need to be in control, to know the outcome and to anticipate it, almost as if he was trying to reverse the lack of control and terror he felt in the position he occupied within the family. To be able to exert control over the therapeutic process in an active manner, seemed to be an attempt to regain an active position in his life, even though it manifested itself as a deep preoccupation with death. At moments, X's desire to die appeared to be coming from a deep sense of exhaustion; at others, it felt like there was a desire to seek revenge on those around him, to make them suffer as he had.

X experienced himself as unable to go on with life, bound to fail at it by design, as though he had drawn the losing hand. He would press for quantitative assessments, in an attempt to prove his hypothesis, of not being good enough. His first attempt took place at the young age of 18, when he didn't fare well in his entrance exams. After this, he carried a sense of not being good enough, even in his work place, regardless of the fact that he had held a job the entire time we worked together. He felt that he wasn't bright enough or extroverted enough to make it through. No matter which way he looked at the scenario, he felt that he had drawn the short end of the stick. There was no space to reflect on what else he could do, or what he was interested in pursuing. He believed that he had failed because he thought his life was not progressing the way he felt it 'should' be. And that sense of failure remained pervasive. X's critical agency posed a harsh judgement of his capacities and undermined any attempts he made in carrying on in his professional and personal life.

X largely felt hopeless about the world he inhabited both personally and professionally. Yet, he felt that there was a part of him, a child part, that constantly attempted to seek help. It was this part that had brought him to therapy, and glimpses of this part would become more accessible when X would allow himself to be spontaneous or associate freely. He didn't trust this part and felt that he had to control this child part in an attempt to continue with his plan. It was difficult for X to integrate these child and adult parts. This tussle would result in an interruption of any attempts at meaning making or reflection. It appeared that in the absence of having a space for spontaneity and play in his immediate environment, X had constituted a self that was built on an attempt to control the outcomes of situations around him. Though this part would often masquerade as coherent, it was precisely this part that was most affectively distraught, caught between a deep anxiety and an intense rage. While choosing his deadline of March 2018, X had taken into consideration that his father would be retiring from his job and there would be an inflow of money, thus making it the right time. The idea that his death would impact anyone around him remained alien to him. Though he would say this in a matter-of-fact manner, each time he did, I was enveloped in a deep sadness. I began to wonder whether in his attempts to take his life, X was trying to understand whether his existence had an impact on his immediate environment, whether he made a difference, or whether he was even registered as a presence.

To be in the world in itself was a great source of unpleasure for X, and so he sought a painless way to die. Being able to think about a way of ending his life brought X a sense of solace. It seemed to me that he was already in so much pain, pain that was difficult to articulate, that thoughts around an end made the pain bearable. The process of therapy also represented a tussle between pleasure and unpleasure for X. In a certain sense, X took therapy very seriously, he would come on time and never missed sessions. At the same time, in the time between sessions, X would feel a great deal of frustration, making it difficult to sustain coming for therapy, even though he managed to come for each session. It was important for X to maintain that he could terminate therapy at any point, to reduce his frustration. He used therapy 'like a boost', 'a momentary relief' that allowed him to return to being in the world. At the same time, he didn't want therapy to affect his plans of ending his life.

In my work with X, it seemed that he was searching for meaningful connections. He longed for a closeness and felt the need for a 'female anchor' in his life. Apart from home and work, therapy was the only space in which X interacted with someone outside his family and work environment. This need felt deep, and when X had access to it, he felt it important to dismiss it completely or attack the process of therapy. As soon as he would register his attack however, X would become anxious that therapy would come to an end. Unable to pause and reflect on this, X would move to a position of wanting to terminate therapy himself. As if that would allow a measure of control on the process, which remained so important to him. Between attempting to work together in therapy and desiring to work on his self on his own, X expressed a 'desire to be close, a desire to fuse', while at the same time dismissing this as 'over dramatic' or 'just an excuse'. Both separation and mutuality were difficult to tolerate, and X found himself torn between the desire to be and the desire not to be. This tussle would present itself in his preoccupation with death.

I often wondered who X would be, if he wasn't occupying a position of someone on the brink of suicide. He defined himself as having failed at life, not being able to move forward, but found it difficult to elaborate on these statements. They were stated in a self-explanatory manner that often felt empty. It's possible that's how X felt too, very empty, almost hollowed out, making his sense of identity itself a negative, a pre-decided failed coming into being, which could only now return to a prior state, in the hope of containing something alive. In his musings around the desire to die, it often felt like X did not look at death as a finality, where everything ceases to be. For him, it seemed to contain a quality of rest, as if in death, the tussles and conflicts he was navigating would not exist and that was a peaceful image, pulsating with a sense of being alive.

P's Case

P came for therapy because it was an option in the university space. He seemed curious about the clinic and wondered if it could help him. When P was assigned to me, what struck me most was, once again, the referral form, which read: 'lots of pain in my mind. I want to sleep for a long time. Confusion. Irritation. I am not being able to manage my life (mind).' The way he had bracketed the mind as different from life, and yet not too far apart, made me wonder what P's relationship was to being in the university. P was not the first university student I had been assigned, and having worked with a few by then, I thought that P was trying to negotiate the transition into university life. This was not an uncommon thing for younger students who came to the clinic. However, the nature of work was usually a little different. It would involve being more actively responsive and mentoring, rather than interpreting and analysing. At least, that had been my experience.

It wasn't difficult to set up an appointment with P. He was prompt to respond and accepted the first slot I offered. P was on time for our first meeting, but didn't walk in to the clinic. He sat patiently outside and waited. He thought he would be called in when I was ready. The guard encouraged him to go and ask, but he decided to wait. Inside the room, I wondered why P was late and as I stepped out to check, I found him sitting outside. I invited him in and he walked in, holding his bag in front of him. His voice was soft and shaky. I enquired how long he had been waiting. He informed me that he had been there on time, but hadn't been sure if he should just walk in. I clarified to him that whenever an assigned time is given, he can feel free to walk in, and that I would be here at that time too. He nodded. It seemed to me that P was uncertain of this space, what it could do, or who I was.

P found it easier to speak in Hindi and wondered if that was okay. He took some time to start talking. There seemed to be a lot going on in his mind and as he began to talk about it, he couldn't stop crying. *'Bahut dard hota hai mujhe. Bahut dard.'* (I experience a lot of pain. A lot of pain). He was struck by a sense of pain, and felt it emanating the most from his head. It had been there for a while, but P was beginning to feel like it had become unbearable. He just needed the pain to end. As he told me a little more about himself, he struggled to talk about his family. He was the middle child of three siblings, and felt that he wasn't being able to match up to what was expected of him. At moments, he experienced himself as 'lesser than' and weak, owing to his physical frame as well. P had been bullied a lot in school, and recalled how it got better when his father paid a visit to the school. He seemed preoccupied with how people interacted with each other. His experiences made him believe that in interactions one was always putting the other person down. Watching this, and experiencing it, gave him a deep sense of pain. Sometimes, he felt like the only way of dealing with the pain would be to end his life, though he had never attempted to do so. The need to sleep for a long time, and the sense of confusion and irritation seemed to be stemming from this pain. His expectations from therapy were *'ki kisi na kisi tarah se yeh dard kum kardo'*. (somehow, in some way, reduce this pain). As I heard him say this, I felt deeply affected. He felt frail to me, and the burden he carried seemed immense.

Reaching the university was a distinctly different experience for P; it was different from the spaces he had been in before. He recounted how in school he constantly felt frustrated, because the teachers wouldn't come to teach. He would struggle with his academics from time to time. However, there was one teacher who supported him through his struggles, and though he felt thankful for that, his pervasive sense was that of an intense amount of pain. He wasn't able to talk about this pain to anyone at that point, but now felt more ready to talk about it with someone. *'Mujhe dard main nahi rehna, yeh dard khatam he nahi hota, aur kuch isse kum bhi nahi kar paata. Kabhi kabhi lagta hai ki baat karne se shayad help ho, isliye maene socha yahaan aa jaon.'* (I don't want to live in pain, this pain doesn't end and nothing reduces this pain. Sometimes I feel that maybe talking about it might help, that's why I thought I'll come here). I felt a deep sadness when P said this, but also felt hopeful that he was being able to acknowledge his pain as important and worth seeking help for.

P talked about how he constantly felt 'crazy'. The moments that would impact him and make him feel intense pain, seemed to leave others around him unaffected and apathetic. He recounted an incident in his neighbourhood where two men were in a bad fight and one was brutally beating the other. A crowd had gathered to watch the fight, but no one was intervening to stop it. He happened to be driving by with his father, and was struck by a profound sense of sadness and helplessness. He couldn't stop crying and as he recounted this in the session, he continued to cry. He seemed to be preoccupied with the world around him, its sense of violence and apathy. He brought this up repeatedly in our work together. He couldn't understand why no one was intervening; no one was doing anything to stop or prevent it. This added to his sense of pain. As I heard him talk about this, it resonated with me very deeply. I could feel his anguish and helplessness in these moments, not very different from my own on hearing these instances. On another occasion he said, *'jab mae sochta hu ki humaare desh main hum aurton ke saath kya kartien hai, mujhe bahut dard hota hai. Kya yeh pagalpan hai?'* (when I think about what is happening in our country, what we do with women, I feel a lot of pain. Is this insanity)? He was deeply struck by a horrific rape that had made the headlines at the time. Between witnessing violence and feeling mad, P seemed to be communicating a deep sense of helplessness through his pain. His life (mind) found it difficult to process this disjunct in the absence of a language and a structure. Pain seemed to be its only communication, but he also needed that pain to end as it was becoming too much to bear.

I wondered about the import of these moments on P's internal world, and about how he was making sense of this pain. He seemed to be looking for a language to articulate this pain and to be able to communicate it. In his classes he would, sometimes, feel disheartened. What he was being taught was different from what he was experiencing. He wondered why he wasn't being taught something more current that would allow him to understand what was happening in the world right now, or what he was going through. Initially, he felt like this was an isolating experience; academics felt distant, because it was in a different language, both structurally and emotionally. At these moments, writing would help. He had begun to write poetry, in Hindi and in English.

Poetry became an important intermediary space for P, and an easier way to communicate what was going on inside. P began to share his poetry with me and with some of his friends. His poetry carried both a personal and an impersonal quality to it, bringing together what he was seeing in the world, and the anguish it was making him experience. P *felt* deeply, and writing about it allowed him to externalize some of that feeling. His belief was that talking about these things was also in the service of the same. At moments when his poetry was responded to, P felt confused. These were moments of recognition, but also moments of departure for him. It was difficult for him to navigate what was being seen in his writing, as if the experience of being seen in itself was a confusing experience for him.

As the work continued, P began to talk more about being in the university. He had started get involved in university activities of all kinds. He was trying to build a community for himself, closer to his present experience, rather than the one he came from. The struggles that he had seen, and the ones he was experiencing within the space, were being navigated, both by coming to the clinic and finding other facets of the university that were designed to aid students.

There was a deep kindness in P that made him more open to what others around him seemed to be experiencing. In one of our sessions, P seemed distracted while talking. His phone was constantly ringing and he would keep glancing at it, as if wondering if he could pick it up. After a couple of missed calls he finally said, *'exams chal rahe hai na aur mera dost pareyshaan ho raha hai. Usse kuch samjhna tha, iske baad mae waheen jaane wala hu. Shayad kuch zyaada hi paryeshaan hai, mae abhi jaaun?'* (Exams are going on and my friend is very troubled. I have to explain something to him, after this, I will go there. Maybe he's a bit too troubled. Should I go there now)? It seemed more urgent for him to go and attend to his friend, than to himself: *'aise haalat main kisi ko akela nahi chordna chahata'*. (In this situation I don't want to leave anyone alone). In the session that followed, he was concerned about how I must have felt about him leaving the session midway. He was concerned that I might have taken it badly or wouldn't have understood it. He explained, in some detail, how important it was to be there for his friend. This was important for P, as though taking care of this friend was also a way of taking care of a part of his self that felt similarly. I responded to his concern about my feelings by saying, *'Mujhe bura nahi laga kyunki aap waapis bhi toh aaye, aur hum iss baare main baat kar paa rahe hai.'* (I did not feel bad because you also came back and we are being able to talk about this). I felt it was important to let P know that these were things that we could return to and process together. It felt important to let him know that this was a place that he could return to, as he was in the process of discovering how to use this space to begin with.

Being from the same university, there were spaces outside the clinic that P and I shared. On one such occasion, he noticed my presence in a protest on caste issues in the university. He wondered about my presence there. *'Aap faculty toh nahi ho sakte, kya aap bhi student ho?'* (You cannot be faculty, are you also a student)? He seemed a bit disappointed with that revelation. As I explored with him what it was like to see me there, he said *'Aapko wahaan aane ki zaroorat toh nahi, aap toh singh ho, mujhe pata hai, bill pe dekha hai, shaayad aap bhi caste samjhna chahte ho, par aap bahut bhole ho. Yeh sab toh kab se chal raha hai aur bahut kuch hota hai.'* (You didn't need to come there, you are a 'Singh,' I know, I have seen it on your bill, maybe you also want to understand catste, but you are very naïve. All this has been going on for a while now and a lot happens). He talked to me about how he interacted with different people and parties in the university, and how he both agreed and disagreed with them. He would feel involved, but also distant when he felt they missed the point. As he tried to create a political stance for himself, he identified a similar struggle in me. This was an important aspect of our work together, as he attempted to bring his political striving into dialogue. He attempted to create a dialogue with me about it, despite our different social locations, which fostered a sense of mutuality between us.

As P's involvement within the university increased, his headaches and sense of pain began to reduce. Though he still remained affected by what was happening around him, P started creating ways to engage with these things, in writing, in conversations, in therapy, and in the positions he occupied within the university space. He wanted to experiment with his new found methods of managing his pain, as he began to experience himself more as an active agent who could also cause pain, instead of a passive recipient of it. As he tapered therapy, he wanted to get a sense of whether he could return to this space, if and when needed. I left that option open for him and he utilized it once. Though therapy, as a process, had opened up a space for P to explore where he was at and how he was feeling, it didn't solve the problem of what he 'should' be doing, what was the 'right thing'. Instead, I attempted to share that struggle with him.

In P, one can see an attempt to symbolize that which feels too much to bear. When we began work together, a sense of 'too muchness' was accessible in his speech and in his breakdowns. Writing seemed to be the first attempt at communicating something he felt at a deeper internal level. In the struggle to formulate his identity, P seemed to be looking for structures to bridge the gap between a part that felt isolated and a part that wanted to be in a community, between retaining links to the community he came from, to creating a newfound sense of community within the university. He began to value what he was saying in class a lot more, and felt that one had to be a part of the system in order to change it. These attempts to strive towards a sense of identity appeared to be efforts to create something beyond the pain, for himself.

In my brief work with P, it felt like he had been trying to understand how to use therapy as a space, while trying to cast me in roles that he had already identified—perhaps as a teacher, as an innocent student with her own struggles, as a woman with her vulnerabilities, and as someone who could (sometimes) understand what he was going through. Therapy became a place where he could talk about what he was experiencing, but it was difficult for him to get a sense of what my motivations were, to sit there, through this experience, with him. Our conversations would, at moments, make me feel a deep sadness for him, while at others, I marvelled at the nature of his mind and thoughts, the deep kindness and compassion he carried, almost against all odds.

In our work together, P's suicidality seemed to be closer to a pre-symbolic state, in the beginning. It manifested as a deep sense of pain and anguish that felt isolating and made him feel 'lesser than'. It made him feel too deeply, which made him feel mad, at times. Parallel to him coming to the clinic, was his striving towards a political identity within the university setting. In between these two spaces, he seemed to be attempting to create ways to deal with, and express, what he was experiencing.

***

It was almost two months after our work together, that I got the news of P's death by suicide. Up until then, I had thought about P as someone who was attempting to negotiate a space between two sides that wouldn't easily come together: a budding political identity and explorations within the clinic. Amid the struggles and pain he carried, and tried to express, there was a part that seemed hopeful, still in the process of forming, still just becoming. The news of his suicide, therefore, hit me like an interruption, a deeply painful one. When I look back at that moment now, it becomes clear to me that I couldn't think beyond my own internal preoccupations at that point. There was fear that I had missed something. I went over all my notes of our brief interaction, hoping I could find something that would explain this moment, reduce this sense of chaos, that may allow me to believe that this could have turned out any other way. The need for predictability and control felt so strong, in that moment, that it took some time for me to see that much of my research question came precisely from this kind of knowingness, knowing that in these moments, the deepest *need* is to find an explanation, and that is precisely the one thing suicide defies, its representation. It is difficult to put to words what the import of this moment was for me, given the facts that P was someone I had worked with, that he wasn't someone who had ever attempted to take his life before, and that I was preoccupied with a research on the same construct. I felt my mind go into a hyperdrive, where sleep didn't feel like a possibility. Moments from our interaction kept returning to me, as did a deep sense of doubt. This had been my 'worst case scenario' while working with suicidality, a scenario that always felt like a very real possibility, but in this moment, how I wished this hadn't been the case.

I felt like I was on very shaky ground, and it became difficult to retain a sense of the narrative of what our interaction had been, given this event. Institutionally, this was a first. And since it was a first, it brought with it, a host of anxieties at multiple levels. There were reports to be made, responses to be given, a line of communication to be established, a clear narrative to be in place, a reflection on procedure to be then articulated. As I recovered from my internal preoccupations, to return to P's death and its impact on those around him, I realized that the ones around me were also wrapped in their internal preoccupations, of how this happened, what went wrong; each person responding not just from their life history, but also a subject position within the university as a space, a space which takes on many characters when it comes to a death by suicide. It was difficult, in that moment, to retain a multiplicity of these subject positions, because to me, the loss felt so deeply personal, despite its impersonal character.

What helped the most, was an initial retreat into myself, to recover the narrative of what had been. It was only after that, that I could return to everything else that had been triggered by this event.

I found myself most concerned with grief intervention for the family, and wondering about what kind of psychological support could be extended to the student community. Given that P was a student of the university, his unanticipated loss would affect the student body in ways that would be difficult to articulate, if not attended to. Everything else felt like noise. Though procedurally significant in its own right, the noise felt so far removed from what had just happened: a life had been lost; a young student, who was someone's child, sibling, friend, confidant, was gone. I found it difficult to stay with individual anxieties of procedures unknown. What seemed paramount to me was a deep sense of loss that I felt needed to be attended to. Despite having a sense of how I would have gone about this, my experience was of not being an agent in my own right. I felt torn between my subject position of being a student in the university and being a trainee within the university clinic. In the multiple anxieties everyone was living, I was fortunate that these concerns found resonance in two senior faculty members, who guided me in the processing of this loss, for I wasn't just the therapist who worked with P, I was also a part of the student community within the university space, who had lost a fellow student.

The visit to P's house to offer our condolences was akin to an out-of-body experience. And yet, everything felt so familiar, not distinct from the reconstructions I carried from our work together. On my way there, I thought about what this journey would have felt like to him, each day, as he made his way to the university; what his thoughts were as he moved between these two spaces, both of which carried their own histories and narratives—could they be brought together? Would that have reduced the pain he felt? As I entered his house, I could recognize, almost instantly, his immediate family members. Members from the community were also present, sharing the loss with P's family, hoping to get a sense of what went wrong. There was great pride in P's achievements within the community. He was one of two people who had made it to a university. Through the entire conversation, the women from the community sat in the background while the men, at the forefront, conducted the conversation. A sense of two distinct communities was apparent as we sat opposite them, clearly separate. P's preoccupation with the plight of women came to mind, and I couldn't help but think about his mother, who wasn't present in the common room, where we were seated. His sister sat at the far back, her eyes a deep red from mourning the loss the family was grappling with. When she was invited to speak, she came and sat next to me. There was something so gentle in her appearance, and my sense was she carried something deep and heavy, which she refused to speak about. There was a pervasive heaviness in the interaction. At a later point in the conversation, I was asked if I would like to meet his mother, who was sitting in a room separate from the common one, on account of not being too well. She seemed disoriented and grief-stricken, asking about her son, not being able to say much more than that, but wanting to extend her hospitality even in that moment. She held my hand gently and asked if there was anything he said that could explain his actions; I had nothing more to offer, except the sheer grief I too felt in this moment. Meeting her left a deep impact on my mind. She felt fragile to me, almost unable to carry the weight of her own body. I constantly thought about how P didn't talk about her much. I wondered if she was absent from our conversations, or made present in the way he experienced his body, as unable to sustain the work it is supposed to be able to do? I felt deeply aware of my own body in this moment, how out of itself it felt and the heaviness it carried, but yet, there was a frame, of language, to carry that heaviness, to be able to articulate it; my sense was P embodied that, but its articulation was interrupted.

A memorial was organized for P, within the university, a month after his demise. His teachers and batchmates spoke about him, and their experience of being with him. Here, the women spoke eloquently about his caring compassionate nature, about his ability to understand other people's pain, about his deep sensitivity. Despite the profound sense of grief that was palpable in the room, all the people he had spoken of at one point or the other during our interactions, were present. They all spoke of his deep capacity to be there for the other, in times of need. As I heard them talk about him, I wondered how he would have felt had he known how deeply he had impacted these people? How much they felt for him and how much his gestures had been appreciated. How in some of their moments of pain, he had been relieving and soothing. How he had made some difference; I imagined him playfully smiling at this, quite confused about the nature of his impact, unaware of his ability to be impactful.

Similar to my experience of being in his house, in this moment too, I could recognize instantly, the people who had spoken about him, what they had meant to him, and the position they occupied in his mind. I felt a deep intimacy, but also a veritable distance, because I knew so much and yet, there was a privacy to this intimacy, and a confidentiality which I felt the need to fiercely protect, then and now. The loss feels so deep, and yet that depth cannot occupy an easy signification, for despite these moments to mourn, I felt outside the circle of mourners, unable to articulate the sheer grief I felt at this loss.

To be a part of this mourning, to think about P, and to truly feel this loss, are part of the process, which is the work of mourning. As a therapist in training at the time, and as a student from a shared student community, preoccupied with larger concerns of being in the university, I, too, had to make room to mourn.

As I write about P, I think it is important to not only give a sense of the life he had lived, with its struggles and triumphant striving towards a formation of identity, but equally important to think about the subject positions and spaces he occupied, the dynamics around them as he attempted to bridge two worlds, that couldn't be easily put together. From the position he came from, to the position he wanted to create and occupy through further education; a position within university spaces, along with being a subject within the clinic. It now becomes even more important to think about P, to reflect further upon what mechanisms can be provided to the students within a university, amid identity confusions and crisis. To better aid and provide a scaffolding to their strivings towards identity.

My work with P was that of a brief support work that lasted 17 sessions. Given his untimely death by suicide two months post our work together, it becomes vital, to my mind, to reflect upon this interaction in an attempt to think about P's movement from suicidality to suicide, albeit speculatively.

***

As mentioned earlier, in P's case, his suicidality appeared to be closer to a pre-symbolic form, manifesting itself somatically, as a sense of pain. He wondered about the plight of women in the society, the nature of caste violence, and other representations of violence, that was discussed in the news. Thinking about all this would make P feel immensely hurt. He wondered about his own being, affected so deeply by this, but on the other hand, thought that it was important to be affected, otherwise one would remain apathetic. But P didn't articulate his thoughts and feelings in this manner. He was in the process of finding representations for it, both in thought and in language. He was more comfortable in Hindi, as I have mentioned before, but the world he found himself in now was predominantly English-speaking. As P ventured towards finding representations for his inner struggles, he became drawn towards different parts of the university structure: he joined the language buddy system to become more comfortable with his use of language; he moved in and out of different political organizations in an attempt to understand where he fit in and what he stood for; and he even brought this dilemma to the clinic to see if talking about what was on his mind would help.

Though P found it difficult to explore the root of his pain, he constantly reflected on the nature of this pain and when he felt it. Being much younger than X and C, P was attempting to straddle two worlds that couldn't be brought together in easy resolution: the world that he had grown up in and the world he now surrounded by. P constantly felt that what he was being taught in the university was different from his experience of being in the world, and wondered about how to use his newfound knowledge. At the same time, P found it difficult to create a space for himself at home and experienced himself as overly affected, and not being able to occupy a clear masculine identity, which at times felt like a requirement, being the older male child, even though he was the middle child of the family. As pointed out earlier, P was the first in his family to make it to a university space. Though this provided P with a new set of opportunities, it also required him to make the most of them.

As our interaction continued, P spoke more about his experience of being in the university and the relationships he had found within the space. He found it important to be there for his peers and friends, so much so that he was willing to leave mid-session if someone he knew needed his help. Though he carried a sense of being different from the people he interacted with, he would respond to their distress and needs. In hindsight, and as I have indicated before, it feels like these were also attempts for him to take care of himself, by actively embodying a sense of care that he didn't feel he had easy access to.

Gradually P's sense of pain began to decrease and he found himself feeling better and being more involved in class, being able to speak up, and make an impression. At moments, he was surprised by the recognition he would get, at other times he would feel a sense of agency and pride about the same. P found different ways to get involved in university life and wondered about the kinds of impact he was able to make on people, in both positive and negative ways. This sense of being able to make an impact was a novel experience for P, though we were unable to gather much reflection around it.

In our work together, P wondered about the position I occupied and who I was. Having shared the university space, he had seen me around but the position of a trainee therapist was a difficult slot to grasp in his mind. There were two possible options—either I was a teacher or I was student. Having seen me in a protest march on caste issues within the university, P was certain that I couldn't have been a teacher. Yet he recognized, in that moment, my own struggles with understanding caste. He was certain that I wasn't from a lower caste, considering he had seen my signature, but felt that there was something genuine in my attempts to understand this location. At that moment, he occupied almost a protective position, concerned that I might be lead astray by the politics; he simultaneously felt that his location would allow him the space to explain some things to me, in a way that could be helpful. Though the moment was an important one of meeting for us, in hindsight, it also feels like a moment where something collapsed. In that moment, both P and I were students within the university, the fantasy of me as a teacher was no longer a possibility, which also meant I no longer had a symbolic authority that might have been useful for our work together. In the months that passed, I have gone back to that moment and wondered had I not been a student as well in P's mind, would it have been easier for him to access help when he needed it the most?

P had terminated work two months before his death by suicide. At the time, when we were bringing work to a close, P had found some spaces of representation for what had felt initially too much to bear. In being part of different structures in the university, in his interactions with his friends and different student groups, P had started finding avenues into this community. Amid all this, he wanted to taper therapy to see how he'd fare, while wanting the option to return in case he needed to, an option he had explicitly been provided and he had availed once.

As I have said before, the news of P's death was a difficult one to process and think through immediately. There remain many gaps between my own understanding of him and what resulted in this step. From the little I have been able to gather, P's suicide carried a degree of impulsivity, which doesn't fit well with my understanding of him. The fact that there wasn't a note or an attempt to reach out, stood out for me, given that P was rather expressive, even if the means of such expression were covert.

My research work was marked by not just the multiple positions of being a student in the university, which is a space of socio-political turbulence, and a trainee in the clinic within the university, but also by another untimely loss, an interruption embodied in P's death by suicide. A loss that definitively changed the trajectory of the present work. And the writing of it is clearly an attempt to process this loss. It is possible to look back now, and wonder, what had been missed in that moment. In attempting to think about that, there is a need to reflect on the processes in the clinic, specifically, a clinic within the university.

At the time, when P was in and out of the clinic, there was also A, who occupied his suicidality in an overt manner, threatening to end his life. It was difficult to take that threat lightly, for there were attempts in the past and a clear plan for the future. That urgency felt so deep that I would take it to every space I could think of, in the hope that it would be addressed, in the hope that there was some help that could be given to A. For now, it feels that something worked, enough to prevent A from taking that step. Perhaps, the work allowed for a space for this suicidality to be engaged with, so that it didn't have to be enacted. And in that, a prevention became a possibility. A was able to reach a space where he could lay claim to the process of therapy, in a way that allowed for these movements; thus, being able to live a kind of *care of the self* through the urgency and threat he conveyed.

On the other hand, P seemed to be in the process of uncovering what care meant. He was able to quickly reach a sense of care and concern for those around him, but remained somewhat unaware of the kind of care *he* desired. Perhaps, a prerequisite for a care of the self would be a sense of what it means *to be cared for*, or what it means *to care*. P seemed to be somewhere in between these two when this interruption took place. For me, this moment will always carry an unknowability. I will never know what happened that day, what troubled him, what he was thinking in that moment. But what nags at me the most, is that I will never fully know, for sure, whether I missed something he was trying to communicate the last time I met him.

This nagging feeling, however, doesn't take on the quality of punitive self-reproach, but instead embodies a cautiousness that now informs my work hereon. P seemed to be doing better, finding different modes of self-expression, moving away from a sense of pain, and wanting to see how he would fair without therapy. Amid this, he moved from finding expression to death by suicide. And that changes the way one looks at the entire work. For now, everything is re-looked at, as if culminating in this moment. Even though that may not have been the case. It is difficult to say, with any certainty, what caused this moment. And there remains a deliberate attempt on my part, to not go into a causality that would allow a simple explaining away. Instead, I have stayed with this moment, gone back to it repeatedly, in the hope that something more could be recovered, not just for P, but for many others like him. Though there is nothing I would do differently about the work we did together, what I would add is a mechanism to check in, post-termination.

The adolescent ego requires a space to not only 'inhabit and be inhabited by the body' (Phillips 1993, p. 31), but also requires an 'ideological simplification' (Erikson 1968, p. 27) of the world around it. In an attempt to support this developing ego, I would check in, more actively. Just in case. Though this doesn't ensure a prevention, it does clearly leave a space open, in an explicit manner. Perhaps in a manner that wouldn't escape memory in the moment of crisis. It seems to me, however, to lay claim on that kind of space requires a sense of entitlement. A sense of *I can claim this for myself.* I wonder, in positions of marginality and social otherness, what are the possibilities of being able to reach claim, when the social milieu hasn't provided a space for self-experience?

On one end, there can be attempts to provide care and inclusion. A sliding fee scale to make the clinic more accessible. Reservation to make the university more accessible. But in these moments, accessibility carries a quality of 'from the outer to the inner'; what becomes important to think about, however, is the very nature of this 'inner'. It is here that identity positions, within the milieu, become significant. For the clinician, it would become important to think about what kind of accessibility and care is even a possibility, given a particular identity location.

CHAPTER 4

Understanding Suicidality

Some time had passed between terminating work with the cases presented and the actual writing of this section. This passage of time has been marked by a degree of distance as well, from my own position of trainee therapist in the clinic and of being a student in the university, as I occupy neither of these positions actively at present. Clinical work, in my understanding, is a complex endeavour, a living with and living through of multiple positions and dynamics, especially when the clinic is itself located within a university space. My experience of working with suicidality highlighted the importance of the *here and now*, requiring me to be close to the patient's affect states, closer to the anxiety of what could unfurl, whether it could be contained, what could be done to help, and how to remain present to it. In each of these cases, there were different parts of these preoccupations that got highlighted, different levels of anxiety lived, at different levels of fragmentation. The difficulty of undertaking research, while being preoccupied with clinical work became a reality for me here, as if the two couldn't coexist together, at the same intensity. I believe that tells us something about the difficulty of working with suicidality; it grips the psyche in ways that are difficult to think about, while absorbed in the work. And yet, that absorption is necessary for this work to happen. It demands this. As if the only way to work with suicidality, is to 'take on the delusion that there is no outside, only what is happening in the here and now, within this dyad, in this moment'.[1] As I think about this now, I can see its importance, but in that moment then, my own location of being a student within the university and my life stage being closer to the one occupied by the ones I worked with, didn't easily allow me to take this position. The outside always came in, in shared spaces within the university, in momentary encounters outside the clinic, and sometimes through a lived experience of otherness. It is likely that this research preoccupation that I carried prior to commencing clinical work, impacted it. These two strands sometimes lending themselves to an easy coming together, at other times requiring to be kept apart, so that one could be worked through before the other; though they have never been split apart from each other. Now that some time has passed, I return to C, X and P with a particularity in mind, attempting to reflect upon their lived embodiment of suicidality, and its representation in their narratives; moving closer to the theoretical preoccupations within this work.

Time and distance are useful tools to understand what might have transpired within a dynamic, when one is outside of it. For my research, there was a passage of time between working with these cases and the writing of this section. And now, as I return to this section, two more years have passed. I notice the shift internally, in what had seemed possible then and what has become possible now. While absorbed in training and work, working with suicidality and gathering the resources to do so, I didn't have as much access to what these encounters were doing to me. In unconsciously neglecting this impact, there was valuable information that I lost access to. Yet at the same time, looking back on this now, it becomes clear to me that working with suicidality in itself invites our defences to block the level of distress it creates. It presents a difficult predicament—to not just remain present to the distress in the patient, but to make room for the distress lived and embodied in the relationship with them.

[1] Nagpal, A. and Johri, R (2018) Personal Communication.

Thematic Continuities and the Nature of Transference

Though the manifestation and representation of the nature of suicidality carried its own unique form in C, X, and P's cases, there were some thematic undercurrents that presented themselves as common to all three of them. As I moved out of the university setting, I have noticed a re-occurrence of these themes, particularly in young people who present with suicidality.

The nature of crisis, in each of these cases appeared close to an adolescent stage which brought in an 'urgent need to be helped' (Freud 1958) but wouldn't lend itself to the therapeutic process very easily. As mentioned before, Anna Freud (1958) indicates that 'analytic treatment of adolescents is a hazardous venture from beginning to end.' Since in this stage, the sense of self is constantly in a state of flux, it could become difficult to handle the rapid movements of the patient, from one state to another. Her caution seems to be an important one, given that the libido in adolescence (and in unhappy love affairs and mourning) is already invested in an object it cannot detach its preoccupation from, thus making it difficult for the adolescent to create or sustain a transference in analysis. Though there has been much enactment and movement in the transferrential dynamics in the cases mentioned above, I wonder whether the intensity and the nature of the transference itself was, to some extent, predetermined by my own proximity to their life stage, and hence, unable to lend itself to a depth that might have been important to the work.

In response to this urgent need to be helped, I found it difficult to pause and examine: what is the internal emotional difficulty that the young person wants help with. Between the list of symptoms, the level of distress communicated and the details shared, I felt an information overload and was drawn to the intricacies of what had happened or what could happen. What I missed in this process was what was happening between me and the patient, in the moment. The focus became everything else, but that. Though it was difficult for C and X to access the affective rhythms in their lives, I too found it hard to make room for them. I joined their external focus on events that felt out of their control. In that moment, unaware of my own distress of being in close contact with them, I colluded in ignoring the very real internal distress that was making its presence felt.

For Adam Phillips (1993), the task of adolescence is to 'inhabit and be inhabited by the body' (p. 31). In his understanding, adolescence is a stage where an individual puts its primary holding environment (the body) at risk, in an attempt to develop both a capacity for solitude and for concern. These capacities 'recapitulate something of infancy in a dramatically modified form' (ibid., p. 33). Thus, adolescence serves as a repetition and a reworking of what has been experienced as waiting, love, justice, concern, and quietude, in the stages before. In C's case, it seemed that she was trying to process and master, through the use of her body, moments and feelings that had been difficult to bear and articulate. Her 'craving for love' found a representation through the use of her body, yet inhabiting it (as a site of feeling) remained something C continued to struggle with. X, on the other hand, wanted to find a painless way to rid himself of life, and in doing so wanted a method that didn't harm his body. In my work with X, I began to wonder that if the body has the capacity to house solitude, it could also house shame, anger, hatred, disgust and many other affect states that become difficult to process. If the immediate environment doesn't have a space for their expression, where do these affects go? One possibility is that they find their home, deep within the body. In both C's and X's narratives, the 'generous kind of negligence' (ibid., p. 30) which Phillips states as important for inhabiting the body, seemed to be a difficult sense to reach. Freud (1920) indicates that the ego is first and foremost a bodily ego (p. 3959), and if that is the case, both C and X also appeared to be navigating interrupted moments in the development of the ego, as reflected in the paradoxical positions that they began to occupy.

And yet, a focus on the body, in the moment, during our clinical encounters, escaped my conscious awareness. Though I could notice how the body was becoming central to their reworking of early attachment processes retrospectively, its embodiment within the session remained unexplored. The focus became conscious thought, event and language. This over emphasis on thought is possibly the only way C and X survived their internal distress. This is a mechanism in service of preservation, to allow the ego to exist, despite interruption. However, this mechanism also comes at a great cost, of neglecting the internal conflict and struggle this it bypasses. At that point in my training, I was unable to notice this cost, thus unable to bring it to the young person's awareness. The fear of what could happen did not allow my mind to focus on what *was* happening. Now, this is where I would begin: bringing awareness to the body, in the here and now, and what experiential evidence can be gathered as we talk of events from the past.

While thinking about the nature of suicidality in these cases, the *concept of melancholia* as defined by Freud (1917) would constantly come to mind. What separates melancholia from mourning is a *disorder of self-esteem* (ibid., p. 204) which ends up 'intensifying into a delusionary expectation of punishment'(ibid.). I would often wonder, whether both C and X, and at moments also P, occupied a position of being melancholic, especially in moments where a harsh inner voice would present itself, almost foreclosing possible movements in their exploration of affect. It remains, however, unclear to me, whether there was a loss of the object in both C's and X's cases, or if the possibility of a relationship with a primary object was in itself presented like an impossibility. In both their narratives, there was a 'craving for love', 'a desire to fuse', and 'a desire to be close'. This craving/desire ran so deep, that a great deal of unpleasure could be withstood in the hope that it could be met or actualized. Yet, the constant frustration of not having this fulfilled resulted in a loss of self-esteem in both C and X, such that they were willing to, and at moments also able, to cause harm to the self; as if the self was an active element that had a great deal of control over the situations they found themselves in—the different intimate relationships in C's case and the relationship to the family and immediate environment in X's case. Freud (1917) states that in melancholia, 'the object may not really have died, but may instead have been lost as a love-object' (p. 205). The melancholic perceives the ego to be empty and assumes it to be 'worthless, incapable of functioning and morally reprehensible, he is filled with self-reproach, he levels insults against himself and expects ostracism and punishment' (ibid., p. 206). This eventually results in an 'overcoming of the drive which compels everything that lives to cling to life' (ibid.). In melancholia 'one part of the ego presents itself to the other, critically assesses it and, so to speak, takes it as its object' (ibid., p. 207). Here the ego wants to *assimilate the object.* (ibid., p. 209). As such, a narcissistic type of object choice could indicate a (pre)disposition to melancholia.

In both C and X, there was the presence of a harsh internal critic, who judged, undermined and premeditated their responses to the world around them. It left them feeling lacking, incapable and unable. These old automatic thought processes came in the way of any new healthy forms of relating that they were attempting to create for themselves. This unconscious critical judgement was so pervasive, that at moments it undermined me and any intervention from my end. At the time I was unable to notice how pervasive this impact was. It left me feeling incapacitated to help them, encouraging by design, a passive position from my end. What became neglected in this moment was that part in each of them that had the courage to bring themselves to therapy. No one had brought them in, they were here by their own will and choice. In my work with adolescents at present, I have noticed that this will and choice forms the very basis of the working alliance. Because this will is internal, this part that is capable of making these choices is an internal presence. To build capacity in the developing ego to manage distress, alliance with this part becomes paramount, both for the clinician and the young person.

In all three case representations, there remains an ambivalent *relationship with the mother figure, who assumes a passive withdrawn role, unable to be present* to C, X or P. This absence presence would highlight itself in the process of our work together, in their difficulty in talking about their relationship to the mother, and the ambivalence experienced within the relationship. Though C still succeeded in making a movement towards re-establishing an active relationship with other mother figures and eventually her mother as well, in the case of both X and P, the mother remained conspicuously absent, only made present through her passivity, which presented itself in vulnerable moments. It could be postulated, that these moments of mis-attunement predicated a melancholic self that at times found expression in a movement towards suicidality. Freud (1917) states

> the ego can only kill itself when it is able to treat itself as an object because of the return of object investment, if it is able to direct hostility that applies to the object back against itself and represents the original reaction of the ego against objects in the outside world (p. 212).

Thinking about C, X, and P's movements towards suicidality in this manner, can also allow us to reflect upon their earlier experiences, while also allowing us to decipher what these moments are actually communicating beyond a loss of hope, i.e., rather, a desire to find meaning.

As my therapeutic nuance has evolved, it has become apparent to me that the process of finding meaning requires a co-participant. As a therapist, I will always have access to additional information that the patient may not be able to see, immediately. Not because therapists can read minds but because our training makes accessible a capacity to make links. Whether these links are experienced as meaningful or not, however, only the patient can tell. Because only they know what it feels like to be in the predicament they are in. So for an ambivalent relationship with a primary care giver to predicate a melancholic state, there would be some complex feelings attached to this process.

Unlike the hypothesis of the suicidal self being a psychotic self, I found an exploration through the concept of melancholia more useful in understanding the subject position occupied in a moment of suicidality. In melancholia, the ego feels persecuted by the super ego instead of feeling loved as 'confronted by the massive danger in the objective world that it believes itself powerless to overcome; it sees itself as deserted by all the forces that could have protect it, and lets itself die' (Freud 1923, p. 148). In the hypothesis of psychosis, there is a break from reality such that death becomes an escape. In melancholia however, there seems to be a communication, as if to say that which was expected to be loving and nurturant has been lost; that loss being too much to bear results in a movement towards suicidality, through a process of self-reproach. In the case of C, X and P, the latter hypothesis seemed more useful in trying to open up a reflection on their interaction within their milieu. The question for me wasn't whether there was truth in the sense of loss they carried, 'who' had been lost, or whether the intensity of the craving or desire was justified; the fact that it was there made it valid enough to be explored further. Though there was not much that could be changed about their early experiences, the act of talking about them, witnessing them without questioning them, allowed some space for affect to move, which was useful for our work together.

Within this hypothesis, suicidality doesn't emerge as a break from reality but expresses itself as a communication of an unconscious relational loss. The critic takes centre stage attacking the self for being weak, for having feelings, for not having their shit together. At the same time, there is a part of the self, struggling to integrate and manage these intense feelings. The therapeutic task is to make room for these feelings. 'This is the truth about our early relationships. They are our blueprints. We treat others and ourselves the way we were treated as children. All unknowingly, all because it feels familiar. It is what we know' (Paiva 2017, p. 218).

This further highlighted *the role of the milieu in the creation and sustenance of these states and positions.* Freud (1923) states that the 'ego develops out of identifications which take place of cathexes generated by the id and then abandoned, and that the first of such identifications routinely assume the role of a special judgement entity within the ego, and set about countering the ego' (p. 138). The role of the ego ideal would become important here, especially in understanding the ego alterations around drive. In melancholia however, the object being critically received has been established within the ego through the process of identification such that

> the destructive component has lodged itself in the super ego and then turned against the ego. What thereupon prevails in the super ego is not unlike a pure form of the death drive, indeed it quite often succeeds in driving the ego to its death if the ego doesn't manage to keep its oppressor at bay by switching off (ibid., p. 143).

Since the ego ideal is formed in relation to the outside world and identifications with the same, it would become important for us to give some thought to what it is about this outside world, this milieu occupied by these young people, that seems to be presenting itself close to the death drive itself.

In each of these cases, there appeared to be an attempt to bring together different parts of the self that could not be brought together very easily. As each of them appeared to be in a stage similar to adolescence, a tussle with identity elements and formation also began to highlight itself. In C, this represented itself as a tussle between being a liberal woman, while also maintaining ties to a developing sense of being Muslim. In X, this represented itself through the being and feeling mentally ill. It could be seen in his tussle to be, with a pervasive sense of not being good enough, of having failed in life while still desiring moments of deep association and affective resonance. In P, this represented itself in his attempts to bring together the world he had grown up in and the world he was beginning to inhabit as a student of the university. These parts were usually kept separate from each other, as if they could only exist in contradiction to one another. This need to split, and maintain this split, seemed to function as an attempt to preserve something for each one of them, even though, at moments, this splitting itself seemed to be the problem, constantly creating a sense of conflict and unpleasure.

Even if we could reach moments of thinking about these parts, or reflecting on why they must be kept separate, my sense was that bringing them together remained an impossibility, not just because of the individual nature of conflict, but also because of the social location each one of them occupied. They began to represent a *fractured self* (Bollas, 2018) 'a self divided down the middle, one part that idealized the world and another part that hated it' (p. 29). Between these moments of idealization and hate, there were movements towards suicidality, which seems to be a protest against being deserted by all the forces that were supposed to allow the ego to cling to life. In the case of C and X, though there were preoccupations and moments of suicidality, during the course of our work together, they manifested themselves in more symbolic forms; being able to talk about it, experience it, outside the life of the mind, in the presence of an other, who occupied a position of being open to such conversation, allowed for a space to find representation and symbolization. My sense is that though some amount of destructivity still played itself out, a movement to suicide was deferred, expressing itself more through suicidality, as opposed to the act itself. In P's case however, there seems to have been an interruption in the process of finding symbolization, such that the form it took became the act itself.

While working with these cases, what became significant in my mind was *the roles I was being drawn into in the dynamics of transference and countertransference.* They carried a character particular to me, but established themselves in a position of otherness to the subject. Though these were not roles I identified with, they could be used in order to demarcate and identify a position of otherness. In C's case this presented as a tussle with identifying with being Muslim as other to the Hindu identity I appeared to occupy. In X's case, through an experience of otherness by being close to chronic mental illness in a family member. And in P's case though an identification to being lower caste as other to my being upper caste. Though my experience of these signifiers is more fluid, in the dynamic with each of them, it would produce itself in opposition, and many a time made me think about the difficult question of my own location and what it was doing to the subject. In these moments, this otherness would highlight the limit of my own thinkability and location. Though something affective about these moments could be grasped and worked with, there remained something unknowable, experientially distinct from where I was located. The question of what kind of object I was becoming, within this dynamic, became an important one to reflect upon further.

Andre Green (2005) derives an understanding of countertransference from the drive-object model proposed by Winnicott, which highlights the investment in the object by the child and the role of the object in the process. Green expands on this and states

> the phantasy of the object's response to its proximity precedes and takes precedence over what its objective reaction will be; or more exactly, the relationship between the expectations of the

object's response and this response itself will become the model for the couple anticipation-realisation, producing agreement or disagreement (Green 2005, p. 56).

This model, in Green's understanding allows us to think about helplessness, panic, being overwhelmed, and defences used to cope with trauma by the subject. It is here that he feels the therapist's countertransference can be put on alert and 'must detect, by virtue of a hypersensitive receptivity, the traces left behind by the experience of childhood' (ibid., p. 56). The therapist then embodies reality more directly to maintain the object, and that this 'perception entails a modification of psychic economy; for very often, these patients present a dysfunctioning in their functions of representation' (ibid., p. 53). This task is not as simple as it sounds. While I was in training, I was only able to notice the traces of past experience, retrospectively. Part of the struggle of working with suicidality was precisely this: the presence of the past only became apparent outside the session, while in the session the immediate internal distress was defended against by links to external events.

Though I had not thought about the different locations I have occupied with regard to religion, madness, and caste, in the dynamics with C, X, and P, a pre-decided subject position would present itself, as though, they were more aware of what I could and couldn't do, owing to my location, than I was. Perhaps, in this situation, there is some truth to it, given the oppositional positions within these constructs. What struck me in this moment was that I was already perceived to be a particular kind of other, even if that was not something I identified with. Yet, to have a clear sense of what my own identifications were was difficult to come to immediately, and remains a work in progress. I carried a measure of curiosity whether I really was that Hindu upper caste woman that I was imagined to be. At the same time, not refuting the difference in location provided a space for dialogue around the same, and acted as an ally to the work. With C, even though she felt inhibited in talking about her family and confusions around her religious identity, my acknowledgement of the difference in locations, allowed her to talk from, and own, her location more fully. In that moment I was no longer a judge as to whether she was a good Muslim or not, instead I was a sounding board, a witness to the struggle she was going through. With P, when he saw me at the protest in the university, he highlighted his awareness of our different positions for the first time during the session that followed. Though this difference had been there in use of language and appearance, when it came up through this incident and through acknowledging it and engaging with it, he was able to occupy a position of being an expert, helping me traverse caste in a manner that would not get usurped by the politics that he thought surrounded it. These were moments for me in which the psychological and the social appeared simultaneously. To look at these moments as just one or the other, takes away from the nature of the dynamic I experienced with both C and P.

In attempting to lend a *hypersensitive receptivity* (Green 2005, p. 56), I began to realize that it wasn't just the traces of childhood experience that were finding a representation, but also the nature of a particular kind of social experience, providing particular forms of relating, and distinct subject positions around religion, madness, and caste began presenting themselves. To understand a 'dysfunction in the forms of representation' (ibid., p. 53) we would also have to think about what modes of representation are made available to a particular subject position. Thus, grounding the importance of the milieu in my understanding.

Why the Death Drive?

Freud (1915) defines drive as 'the real motive force behind the advances that have brought the nervous system, with its infinite capabilities, to its present height of development' (p. 16). The difficulty with taking into account the notion of the death drive, or the drive in general, ties closely to the notion of the unconscious which, with its conception, makes a human being a different kind of subject, a subject who is no longer in conscious control. Freud further states that 'drive emerges as a concept on the borderline between the mental and the physical – the psychic representation of stimuli flowing into the psyche from inside the body, or the degree of work-load imposed on the psyche as a result of its relation to the body' (ibid.). The interplay between the psychological and the social becomes an undercurrent in Freud's writing, especially here, where he builds his metapsychology on an interaction between the two.

During the process of the development of the ego, the division and conflict of the drives, differing across different stages of ego development, become another source of unpleasure. The energy in the psychic apparatus is derived from innate drive impulses, but not all these impulses are given access to the same phase of development. Freud states that there are 'numerous occasions where individual drives, or elements of individual drives, prove to be incompatible in their aims and demands with all those others that are capable of joining together to yield the all-embracing unity of the ego' (ibid., p. 48) Though the dominion of the pleasure principle remains in the service of maintaining the unity of the ego, this principle can also be surmounted if the unity of the ego is better sustained through moments of unpleasure. A predicament that seemed to present itself in both the narratives of C and X, where marriage or a preoccupation with taking one's own life seemed to allow the self to remain coherent.

Through Freud, it becomes clear that the drives play an important role, both in the formation of the ego and the ego Ideal, such that a de-mergence and release of destructive energy and sublimation predicate the development of the same. It is only in the case of melancholia, where the ego can take itself as the object, where the possibility of death presents itself, that a tendency towards suicide as an ego modification can be located, as a response to something outside it.

Kernberg (2009), while exploring the concept of the death drive, indicates that 'the death drive runs deeply against more optimistic views of human nature, based on the assumption that if severe frustrations or trauma were absent in early development then aggression would not be a major human problem' (p. 1009). Given that we find ourselves in a world where human aggression and destructivity is rampantly increasing, this view of human nature might actually allow us to further understand and engage with the human potential for aggression, as opposed to assuming that it does not exist or has no connection with the internal world of the patient.

According to Kernberg, '...severely self-destructive psychopatho-logical constellations' (ibid., p. 1017) have indirectly supported the theory of the death drive. In his reading, Freud was led to postulate and reinforce the concept of the death drive through (i) the phe-nomenon of repetition compulsion, (ii) sadism and masochism, (iii) negative therapeutic reaction, (iv) suicide in severe depression (and in non-depressive characterological structures), (v) destructive and self-destructive developments in group processes and their social implications.

While elaborating on the repetition compulsion, Kernberg states that 'the patient engages in an endless repetition of the same usually destructive behaviour that resists the interpretation of assumed and very often well-documented unconscious conflicts involved' (ibid., p. 1012). It has multiple functions and may represent repetition of 'a traumatic relationship with a frustrating or traumatizing object, with the hidden hope that "this time" the other will gratify the needs and wishes of the patient' (ibid., p. 1013). A similar pattern seems to present itself in C's intimate relationships. The repetition compulsion can also represent itself as 'an unconscious effort to destroy potentially helpful relationships out of an unconscious sense of triumph over the person who tries to help, who is envied for not having suffered what the patient, in his mind, has suffered' (ibid.). X's movement from one therapist to another, threatening to terminate work, while dismissing, more often than not, any attempts to help him, could be understood in this light. Though the repetition compulsion can be seen to some extent in C's case and X's, traces of sadism and masochism also present themselves in their relationships with their immediate environment, and within the transference. A negative therapeutic reaction remains a possibility throughout the work between C missing sessions, pausing, and returning for therapy, and X's constant attack in moments of reflection and interpretation. Though such presentation may not carry the severity that Kernberg (2009) is alluding to, it does display a potentiality for the same.

In elaborating on suicidal tendencies, Kernberg indicates that these tendencies can present themselves as a result of a pathology of the depressive position, where 'relentless self-attacks now derived from the internalization of aggressive aspects of the object into the super ego and an attack of the self from the super ego, and the simultaneous identification of the object with the ego or the self' (ibid., p. 1016). This predicament appeared to present itself in X's tussles with suicidality. Such suicidal tendencies are found in non-depressed characters as well, such that 'death emerges as an even elegant abandonment of a depreciated, worthless world' (Kernberg 2007, p. 1016). In this case, suicidality becomes a 'compensatory triumph,' where the position of 'not being afraid of pain or death' is occupied. It is difficult to say if P occupied this position in his movement towards suicide, but this could be one possible way of thinking about it further.

What struck me most about Kernberg's essay was his reading of Freud in understanding self-destructive developments in group processes and their social implications. Through a reflection of Freud's analysis of groups and Vamik Volken's work, Kernberg states,

> there is impressive clinical and sociological evidence for a universal potential for violence in human beings that can be triggered too easily under certain conditions of group regression and corresponding leadership, and that, from the perspective of survival of human societies, may be considered as fundamentally self-destructive (Kernberg 2009, p. 1017).

In the light of the present study, this observation becomes particularly important. Given the location of social otherness occupied by C through her Muslim identity, X through a relationship to madness, and P through being Dalit, a reflection on these positions, with regard to the larger social group becomes important. Its significance highlights itself in the fact that these locations are not just marginalized and in a position of minority, but also are usually at the receiving end of violence and further marginalization in the context of contemporary India, bearing in mind the rise of Hindu nationalism in recent times. In the present social context, non male, non-Hindu, and non-upper caste are threatening positions, where the onslaught of violence and aggression appears to get most triggered. It appears that within the social itself, in the location of the political regime and the interaction between majority and minority groups, something akin to the death drive seems to be presenting itself. In this socio-political context, it appears that, 'the unconscious functions of self-destruction are not just to destroy the self, but, very essentially to destroy significant others as well, be it out of guilt, revenge, envy or triumph' (ibid., p. 1018).

If the rise of suicide rates in India, particularly in these marginalized locations, and the subsequent decriminalization of suicide, represents a negotiation of *cultural ambivalences* (Nandy 1999), the concept of the death drive could shed some light on the nature of self-other relationships that are considered meaningful, while also helping us think about identity elements and locations that are possible to occupy. If suicidality is then understood as a communication, as if to say, that which was expected to be loving and nurturant, has been lost, and it is that sense of loss that brings the subject close to the position of suicidality, it is possible that this communication is not just a reflection of an intra-psychic dynamic, but also an interpersonal one. Here, the interaction of the psyche and the social regain dialogue, most clearly around identity formation, presenting suicidality as a relational problem. 'As all identities are formed in relation to other identities circulating within a culture' (Layton 2007, p. 155), the nature of social inequalities represented through gender, class, caste, religion, would become important points of reflection to understand 'wounds that split the psyche creating shameful vulnerabilities which we defend against by wielding identity as a weapon against others' (ibid.).

To further understand representations of suicidality and suicide, it would become important to think, therefore, about the relationship between the ego and the ego ideal which represents itself more clearly in the formation of identity.

Identity and its Crisis

Erik Erikson (1968) understands identity as a formulation that 'bears such a definitive name [but] remains subject to changing historical connotations' (p. 15). In his understanding, identity positions and locations are a product of historical and social change, such that these positions change with the times and evolve with the culture they are steeped in. His conception of 'identity crisis' is a psychosocial attempt to understand meaningful modes of relating that are present for the adolescent in particular, who begins the quest of formulating a coherent sense of identity. Since adolescence, as a stage, has been marked as significant in the cases I worked with, the struggles and tussles around identity experienced by C, X, and P, could also help us reflect on the present historical moment. For Erikson '...to discuss the identity problem, then, and to describe its dimensions at the very time when we clinicians are listened to, means to play into cultural history, or, perhaps, to become its tool' (ibid., p. 27).

Erikson (1968) foregrounds the significance of the social milieu, and the times the subject is present in, by looking at the possibilities of identifications and the roles made available at a given time, within a given community. The social then becomes an important fact not just in the constitution of the subject, but also in the position made available for the subject to occupy. A historical crisis however, forces *radical selection* in the adolescent ego's attempts at bringing together different identity elements. Ego development, as a process, does not take place in isolation, and its modification and growth are contingent on a complex interaction between the inside and outside of the psyche. The first modes of identification develop the ego Ideal, which also forms a representation of meaningful modes of identification present in the subject's milieu. To be able to get a sense of an integrated identity, which Erikson terms 'Ego Identity', there has to be a 'subjective aspect, in the awareness of the fact that there is a self-sameness and continuity to the ego's synthesizing methods, the style of one's individuality, and that this style coincides with the sameness and continuity of ones meaning for significant others in the immediate community' (ibid., p. 50).

Through working within the clinic, I began to realize that in an attempt to gain a sense of identity with a sense of self sameness, individuality, and meaning for significant others, the subject's ego was willing to withstand a great deal of flux, conflict, and unpleasure. The sense of identity crisis remained most pervasive in C's case, the only resolution of which was a return to modes of relating that were considered meaningful within her community. I began to wonder how a social location begins to define which identity elements can be brought together and which cannot, the balance between individuality and immediate community being a difficult one to traverse.

In P's case, this struggle for identity appeared in a sharp manner, where a deep tie with either identity (where he came from and his location in the university) had not yet established itself. P was attempting to grasp identity elements that occupied conflicting positions in his mind. Coming from a Dalit family, and being the first to be exposed to higher education, presented itself with a different set of questions about the self, its location within his community, and its interaction with larger social institutions. In the university, he attempted to find spaces that would bridge the gap between where he came from and a sense of self that was developing. From having a difficulty with language, to becoming a tutor for the next batch, to being involved in caste struggles and their representation within the university structure with a personal sense of an ethics of politics, P seemed to be in the process of identifying elements that he could bring together. A coherence around them hadn't developed yet, and it seemed that neither had a sense of individuality. Though struggles with these elements might be seen in any location or community, his struggles in particular however, highlight, in my understanding, something particular to the community he belonged to. The task of identity development presents itself in an uphill manner, carrying with it a history of violence and marginalization that is difficult to surpass quickly, and might require a special engagement to understand what kind of *ideological simplification* (Erikson 1968, p. 27) would become necessary for this subject position. Erikson indicates that for a sense of 'inner identity' the individual 'must feel a progressive continuity between that which he has come to be during the long years of childhood and that which he promises to become in the anticipated future' (ibid., p. 87). The question for us then becomes: how to lend a space to this sense of continuity which in itself appears to be a privileged position, especially for marginalized social positions?

Paul Verhaeghe (2012) highlights the role of the environment in the formation and development of identity. In his understanding, there is no inherent identity and whichever identity is made present or occupied is a reflection on the environment around it. Extending this, we could also postulate that identity locations are a reflection of our social and cultural milieu, the latter determining the possibilities of who we are. In Verhaeghe's understanding, 'we determine our identity by placing it alongside and increasingly contrasting it with other identities' (ibid., p. 11). This process presented itself to me in the dynamics of transference and countertransference in all three cases, such that a reflection on my own identity in contrast to the one occupied by the subject became important. Further, he states,

> right from the start, our identity is a balance of tensions; we are torn between the urge to merge and the urge to distance ourselves from the other. That's because, alongside and intermingled with the initial process of identification and mirroring, there is also a second process at work: a striving for autonomy and thus separation from the other (ibid., p. 10).

The nature of this conflict presents itself in a paradoxical fashion, establishing the desire to be close and the desire to separate in a tussle with each other. If we think of this at the level of the drives, in the attempts to merge and mirror, there is an expression of the life drive, a 'mergence' of it, through the other. While in the attempts to separate and differentiate, there seems to be an expression of the death drive, through de-mergence from the other. But since these two present themselves together, it is difficult to tease them apart. The interplay between them becomes important to the formation of identity. Bringing together these conflicting contrasting parts then becomes the process of identity formation such that 'we are all unique because we have been exposed to different mirrorings and have made our own choices. And yet to a degree we are identical, because the mirrorings of particular groups and particular cultures are to a great extent shared' (ibid., p. 18). To understand identity then, the task for the clinician or the researcher becomes to engage with uniqueness and culture simultaneously, reflecting both on the nature of the representation brought in by the subject of the clinic and what it tells us about the milieu s/he occupies. While attempting to engage with suicidality, struggles with identity development and formation became an important link to further elaborate the nature of individual distress and highlight the struggles within a community at its location in the present cultural context.

Reflections on the University Clinic

The role of identity finds significance in this work also owing to the setting this work is placed in. The university allows for a coming together of different sections of society, with different aspirations, histories, and marginalities. In parallel, the setting of the university also locates itself within an urban environment, while making it accessible to those outside it. It represents a structure that makes possible a movement between tradition and modernity, while also providing a reflection on one's own subject positions, especially when it is a liberal arts university. It offers the possibilities of new identity formations based on the navigation of transitions and conflicts, coming close to the life stage that the subject might be located in. In that sense, the university becomes instrumental in the navigation between the inside-outside of not just the space the subject is coming from, but structures of group, family, and socio-economic location as well. As a sense of self begins to develop, a sense of what is other than the self, Other to the self, also becomes demarcated in these moments. Both inclusion and marginalization become apparent as multiple subject positions are made available through critical reflection and engagement. From language of communication and pedagogy of education, to an ethic of care of the self and the other, the university exposes the subject to a sense of crisis: 'a loss of personal sameness and historical continuity' (Erikson 1968, p. 17).

C and P's cases embodied this sense of crisis, which often presented itself through oppositional elements that remained in conflict with each other. It seemed as though their locations did not lend to an easy representation. Their being in the university space appeared to present some positions as a possibility within the space, but not outside it. A similar predicament presented itself in my own sense of self, where the possibility of being a student, while also being a trainee psychotherapist, presented itself in contradictory ways, where occupying one position meant not occupying the other. To be both fully was an impossibility.

As I observed these transitions, both as someone working in the university clinic and as someone who has been a part of the university as a student, I noted that there seemed to be a gap—between a need being experienced by the student, and the expectation of its reception, on their part, from the institution. A gap that would, at some moments, result in protest or complete breakdown of communication. Identity locations on both ends appeared to be in opposition to each other, which require a separate reflection. It is possibly in moments like these, that Rohith Vemula's suicide becomes an important signifier of the struggles in the university space.

The highest number of suicides in our country are taking place currently in the university space and seem to find a representation around struggles with identity. My sense is that in an attempt to engage with this increase in suicides, one would have to think about the nature of identity crisis within the university as a space for education. A reflection on the nature of pedagogy would become important here, especially in the formation and development of an ego identity. Erik Erikson (1968) states that 'education for an ego identity which receives strength from changing historical conditions demands a conscious acceptance of historical heterogeneity on the part of adults, combined with an enlightened effort to provide human childhood everywhere with a new fund of meaningful continuity' (p. 71). To account for social change, social locations, and create a combined effort, the structure of the university would require a deep engagement with these changes, an awareness of the milieu it finds itself in, and the context we live in. To deny the flux of the current socio-political climate, or to consider it irrelevant and only political, appears to be a way of not engaging with the historical moment the university and the student find themselves in. To only intellectualize it, in theory, and not engage with its affective residue maintains a split between thought and affect, making the situation bearable only temporarily, creating new symptoms and manifestations. Perhaps, the increase in suicidality is one of them. A clinic within the university then, would benefit from trying to bring together these parts that appear to be splitting.

Understanding Suicidality

In engaging with suicidality, I found it difficult to leave behind the social or not to let it in; it always found a representation. Working with it, avowing it, and engaging with it, allowed some space for a dialogue to start; though my sense remains that these concerns cannot be contained within the clinic alone. While working with X, there was still a semblance of a setting that could be maintained despite his deep preoccupation with taking his own life. Here, the parameters of clinical work appeared to be clearer. But while working with both C and P, the nature of social otherness, the history of violence and marginality this carried, and the opposition it established itself in through my own identity location, became difficult to brush past or resolve. This is not to say that the clinic within a university cannot work with social otherness or marginality, but it must acknowledge the nature of this otherness or marginality as beyond its immediate resolution.

Both within the university setting and outside it, I have discovered that in engaging with suicidality among the youth, an attempt to bridge the split between the psyche and the social becomes important. Christopher Bollas, in his book *Meaning and Melancholia* (2018), states that,

> the aim of borderline splitting is to allow both states of mind to coexist in the same personality without ever communicating with one another. When society divides in accordance with borderline logic, the split generates the extreme views on both sides, making it impossible to communicate even though both views co-exist within the same "body" (p. 123).

To begin engagement then, I believe a psychosocially informed clinical space has been more helpful.

To engage with suicidality—its expressions and communications—it becomes important to think about the nature of the social and meaningful modes of relating that are made available in the particularity of this historical moment. It was a reflection on the historical moment of war and violence that resulted in Freud's conception of the death drive. I believe that we find ourselves in a similar predicament today, where the concept of the death drive opens up the possibilities of human destructivity, while also providing a model to engage with it.

Bollas attempts to make sense of this rise of destructivity within the context of what he calls the western civilization. In his understanding, psychic states are shared by societies and 'when a state of mind is the outcome of an unchanging and prolonged situation, it may no longer be experienced as a mood' (ibid., p. xx). He defines this state of mind as an *unconscious axiom* (ibid.) which forms the organized structure of mentalities. Further, he states, 'To understand the psychosocial crisis of the modern world it is imperative to grasp the power of these transgenerational axioms' (ibid., p. xxv). What we see as a manifestation now, is a representation of what has not been addressed earlier, carried forward generationally in the evolution of the human. In Bollas's reading, through the great war, rapid industrialization, the growth of technology and liberalization, the nature of the human has undergone a change, as have the modes of relating and meaning making.

In our context, colonization, imperialism, partition, globalization, growth of technology, and the rise of a right-wing government, might be indicating the same. Though the nature of these trajectories is different for the west and the global south, what appears to be in common between both is the rise of hostility, destructivity, and inter group hate. Ideology exists in contradiction to the basic ethic of being human, such that a care of the self can result in the annihilation of the other, without consequence. This indicates that there has been a deep split established between the positive and negative parts of the self. Bollas further elaborates, '…keeping in mind the structuralization of conflict, in which the original dynamic unconscious formation of a mental or cultural position develops into an axion that has lost any link with its origins, the borderline solution will successfully keep apart radical contradictions between ideological positions' (2018, p. 33).

This has fostered a *fractured self* through which 'it seems that we are provided with many vehicles to help us eliminate the pain of being a subject, and the integrity of thought that supports the illusion of a coherent 'I' (ibid., p. 65). In this loss of link, there has been a loss of continuity with the historical, such that a certain kind of destructive potential, within the human, presents itself parallel to notions of growth and development. The two do not speak to each other. Unlike an existential reflection done by Camus in *The Myth of Sisyphus* through which he concludes that 'it is legitimate and necessary to wonder whether life has a meaning; therefore, it is legitimate to meet the problem of suicide face to face,' (ibid., p. 27), there seems to be a suspension of thought and engagement. It is here that *subjecticide* becomes a possibility, where the

> self suffering from profound oppression will reveal impoverishments of thinking and affect. This can be understood as a form of mental suicide, or subjecticide, which offers the self an ego position in the new social order through the elimination of sophisticated forms of perception and thoughtfulness (ibid., p. 69).

The world we live in is moving towards simpler forms of understanding, while technology is advancing at a rampant pace, and altering the nature of human-to-human contact. The COVID-19 pandemic has only compounded this situation further. If our endeavours to understand suicidality do not take into account the nature of the times, the flux in the social, and the manifestations of the destructive capacities within the human, the risk of subjecticide runs deep, not just in the individual but within institutions as well. This 'desire for ridding complexity and moving towards simplification' (2018, p. 77), reflects for Bollas a manifestation of the death drive: 'a self's retreat from a non-familiar world into an enclave secluded for the self. Juxtapose this to the life drive, in which selves invest in multiple and diverse objects that enable them to expand their interests and radiate their potential in creative ways' (ibid., p. 78).

However, it is important to state that such reflection, or engagement, with these particular concepts is not the only way to understand suicidality and its representations. This work, in that sense, is an attempt to bring together parts of my own experience, as a trainee in a university clinic and a student in the same university, at a time when there remains considerable socio-political turbulence in the spaces I have occupied. My own positions within this work, in the clinic, in the university, and subject to my own life history, have been entry points and attempts at engaging with suicide and suicidality. Psychoanalytic thinking, as I have understood it, has provided the flexibility to occupy a particular position, a conceptual framework, and a metapsychology, to respond to a set of questions. This work occupies one such position, in an attempt to see what the possibilities are, from this vantage point.

Epilogue
Suicidality: A Relational Problem

The problem presented by the rising rates of suicide among the youth in India is not a new problem. For some time now, those of us who work with emotional distress have been noticing the signs. There has been a steady rise in mental health concerns in India. In 2018, *Times of India* reported that 'India is the 6th Most Depressed Country' citing a WHO report. It went on to say: 'The report also threw light on another disturbing fact. Almost 80% people diagnosed with mental sickness do not seek any kind of treatment and there are 150 million more who need access to therapy and this is projected to increase by 20% by 2020' (TNN, 2018).

Though a projected rise in mental health concerns has steadily been in the pipeline for a while, no one could have anticipated the unprecedented impact of the pandemic. For the first time, a democratic country with a population of more than 1.3 billion people, went into a nation-wide lockdown. In a preventive measure to curb the spread of COVID-19, India initially announced a 21-day lockdown on 24 March 2020. This overnight measure threw the country into chaos with a mass exodus of migrant populations, confusion about lockdown execution and protocol, and questions about implementation and safety measures. Parallel to these external concerns, there was an internal emotional roller coaster of uncertainties, insecurities and anxieties that got set off. With no clear end in sight. Those fortunate enough to have roofs over their heads, were locked in. While others risked their lives, their livelihoods and their kin's lives to get 'home'. At that point, not much was known about COVID-19. And yet, this unknown entity presented an unprecedented threat to the world as we had known it.

As we make our way back to a 'new normal', the impact of the pandemic, the lockdown, the political climate and the changes in our institutional structures continue to impact our ways of being in this new world. In this period, despite our collective denial of emotional distress, symptoms of their impact began to surface.

When not attended to, the emotional world has a way of making its presence felt. Because our feelings are a force of nature, much like the wind or the rain, pretending they don't exist, does not work. We cannot expect the sexuality and aggression of youth, which fuels their creativity and desire to change/rebel against the world, to simply quieten down and comply. Distress accumulates, it pushes through and we are forced to notice it' (Paiva 2020).

In my work with young people in the university setting and outside it, the presence of emotional distress predated the pandemic. The pandemic has only compounded an already complex situation. To engage with this rise in emotional distress and suicidality, it is important for us to acknowledge the presence of a complex internal world in each individual and its relation to the external world it occupies.

The problem of feelings is a real threat to our thinly veiled denial of reality. Our internal responses to the world we inhabit make us who we are. At the same time, these responses can pose a threat to our significant relationships when they don't comply to the order of things. Developmentally, for the adolescent, feeling a feeling in itself is an amplified experience. Feelings, when ignored by the immediate environment, become a dangerous entity, best to be warded off and avoided by thought. The only problem, however, is that these feelings are not going anywhere and eventually express themselves in volatile ways. The young person is then left incapacitated, in the face of internal distress. Seeking support, help or aid in these moments is usually difficult. It is not unsurprising that most of us do not even notice our internal distress, in the absence of an external event. The pandemic, in that sense, has forced us to look inwards. And despite that, there are some who muster up the internal strength to seek out a relational engagement.

If we don't quickly jump to classifications, disorders and labels and make room for our complex emotional worlds, we would have to take notice of what these symptoms, rising rates of depression, anxiety and suicide are communications of.

There is little scientific evidence to support the claim that depression is a genuine medical illness that causes suicide. Advocates of this position confuse correlation with causation because so called depression, like suicidal feelings, is just another set of symptoms of psychological distress. The great disaster of this myth is that once the professional assumes that depression is the cause rather than just another symptom, they then look no further for whatever the real causes, are. And then, typically, they resort to the biological 'solution' of drugs rather than addressing the psychological, social and spiritual roots of these feelings (Webb 2013).

Durkheim (1876), in his analysis of suicide, established its increase as a reflection of the problem of modernity. In his understanding, dramatic social change impacts both the individual and the group, making some more susceptible to suicide than others. Through his theory, he gives a typology of suicide based on two axes: integration which is 'the sense of belonging and inclusion, love, care, and concern that can flow (or not flow) from social ties' (Wray et al. 2011, p. 507) and regulation which is the 'monitoring, oversight and guidance that come from social ties' (ibid., p. 508). Since both integration and regulation are relational responses to social ties, the rise in suicidality could also be signalling a collapse of social ties, highlighting once again the interplay between the psyche and the social in the movement towards suicide. 'Only when these forces are balanced, when the individual feels at harmony with their own needs and the demands of the group, does the suicide rate diminish' (ibid. 2011, p. 509). As mentioned before, moments of suicidality could thus be understood as a communication that, that which was supposed to be nurturant, has been lost. To return from that sense of deep loss, making room for the feelings created by this loss and creating a scaffolding to engage with the same become important. Though a sense of balance and harmony may be difficult to achieve in the present socio-political climate, engaging with it might offer the space to acknowledge this loss, to give it some form of representation and meaning, in the hope that acting this out or embodying it could be deferred. By approaching the communication of suicidality with compassion and making room for the mixed feelings it creates, we come face to face with that which has been defended against. Interrupted ego development in the individual can then be provided a space to build its capacity to tolerate these feelings, experience them and move past them.

Through Durkheim, we can conclude that fluctuations in suicide rates arise out of a disruption within the integration and regulation axis. This presents itself in a manner as if the young person is demanding more than the milieu can provide for. In this moment, what can be provided for, will in itself be a product of the nature of that milieu. So, the identity positions and locations that are made available to a developing adolescent ego will be representations of a particular historical moment, with its specificities. It could be postulated, that a moment of suicide is, as if, a communication that the different parts of this identity could not be reconciled. Perhaps, under these circumstances, suicide would become a self-defence, not a self-destruction; an attempt to preserve the true self, which has been denied an expression. Winnicott (1960) postulates that in a movement that leans towards health, if the False Self cannot create conditions for the True Self to come to its own, 'there must be recognized a new defence against exploitation of the True Self, and if there is doubt then the clinical result is suicide' (p. 142).

In an attempt to understand the nature of this exploitation, an engagement with the possibilities provided by the socio-political became important while engaging with suicidality. To make room for this, however, does not mean negating the struggle and suffering endured by the individual, but expanding the space to engage with the nature of the human condition, in the present moment. To this avail, the case representations presented within this work have been reflected on with particular emphasis on the concept of the death drive. The death drive, as seen during the discussion of the three case studies, finds clinical representation in the compulsion to repeat, the play of

active-passive, masochism, and melancholia. Thinking through the death drive has shed some light on the nature of self-other relationships that are considered meaningful, while also helping us think about identity elements and locations that are possible to occupy. If suicidality is understood as a communication, as if to say, that which was expected to be loving and nurturant, has been lost, and it is that sense of loss that brings the subject close to the position of suicidality, it also becomes possible that this communication is not just a reflection of an intra-psychic dynamic, but also an interpersonal one. Thus, bringing together a tussle between self-care and the world-view the young person comes from. The concept of the death drive allowed me to engage with the nature of the social, as represented in individual life histories. Tragically, in P's case, the concept of the death drive brought together caste and its relationship to the increase in suicide rates, such that the destructive pull towards this representation could be further elaborated.

For a psychotherapist, while engaging with suicidality, it becomes important to respond to the specificity of experience that is being brought into the session. This embodied experience presents a glimpse of the times it expresses itself in. To engage with it then, it would become important to reflect not just on the nature of individual suffering, but also their interaction with relevant socio-political forces. The daunting task for the therapist is to acknowledge the real threat of suicide while making room for the feelings underneath it that precipitate it. The young person who brings themselves to therapy while experiencing suicidality deserves special mention. As much as suicidality is an internal experience of dread, despair and hopelessness, in bringing themselves to therapy, the young person also brings that part which has a capacity to notice that something doesn't feel right. In noticing that internal discomfort, even if there isn't much language around it, the evidence of the presence of a part that is not suicidal is acknowledged. A conscious alliance with this part is essential to making room for suicidality.

While I was in training, the threat of what suicidality could do to the subject remained at the forefront of my engagement with my patients. This is a very real anxiety that should not be taken lightly. At the same time, it must not be the only guiding principle to working with suicidality. I now know, making room for this anxiety is a part of the process of working with suicidality. The therapist must create a circle of care not just for the young person, but also for themselves, both professionally and personally to make space for this distress.

The honest truth of the matter is that if someone wants to end their life, they most certainly can. But if that is the only thing they wanted to do, they would not seek out a therapeutic encounter. It is this conflict, the feelings underneath it, and the different parts of the self that the young person unconsciously presents with, that need to be brought to awareness—by helping them notice it, make room for it, engage with it, if they feel willing to do so.

It is important to maintain a non-judgemental and open attitude to talking about these thoughts and feelings. All too often, therapists assume that talking about suicidality could precipitate it. There is no evidence to substantiate this claim but yes, once suicidality has been communicated, there are a host of feelings and anxieties that get triggered even in the therapist. The therapist, like others in the relational dynamic with the young person, is not immune. It is important for the therapist to take note of and attend to this anxiety outside the therapeutic setting—in their supervision processes with senior colleagues, peer supervision and self-work. In acknowledging the anxiety of suicide, the therapist is able to make room for other parts of the young person, in their minds, to make their presence felt, within the session.

This is especially hard for early career psychotherapists because working with suicidality also forces us to engage with our most vulnerable parts and the feelings evoked within. It shatters the myth that the therapist has control or is the expert. I found it difficult to access my own anxieties while I was training. My own internal critic, activated within the dynamic with a young person, followed me outside it. I felt incapacitated to help and judged myself harshly for not knowing what to do. There was clearly a fantasy that as a psychotherapist in training,

I must 'know'. As time passed, I began to understand the nature of this enactment. In denying my own internal responses, I was unconsciously mirroring the young person's internal plight. I had identified with their projection of will and begun to believe, like them, that the answers to this internal difficulty could be sought externally. In avoiding my own internal world, I was unable to make room for these feelings. This is possibly why we avoid talking about suicidality. It is evocative, anxiety-provoking and dreadfully painful. It doesn't lend itself to easy resolutions. So we avoid it, dismiss it, minimize it, even pretend like it's not there. But the feelings underneath this symptom do not just disappear. Making room for this impact in my spaces of support and care has enabled me to notice the nature of this enactment with the young person and bring it to conscious awareness. The young person can then have a choice—are they willing to make room for these feelings?

I have found it useful to never assume that I 'know' what the young person means when they say they feel suicidal. The multiple problems with definitions and classification have been elaborated in the earlier sections of this work but even if we put these aside, you cannot 'know' what the young person 'feels'. These feelings have been carried by the young person through their network of signification and life history. Only they can know what they are feeling, where they feel it and how this feeling came to be. They are the expert on their life and sometimes stating just that is enough to open a space for dialogue. A shared understanding of the experience of suicidality or examples in which suicidality presents itself facilitates a collaborative approach between the therapist and the young person, thus inviting the latter to observe, experience and understand themselves better.

As I continue to engage with Suicidality, there are many positions that I have occupied, apart from the therapist. As a friend, a family member, a fellow student, a witness and survivor. None of these locations make it easier to bear witness to suicidality or a loss to suicide. Which is precisely why engaging with it becomes so important. At the base of it, suicidality is a communication of internal emotional distress. It is a response to our interaction with the world we inhabit, the identity elements made available in a given historical moment. It is a relational problem. To engage with it then, we need to begin with the permission to have feelings and to have conflicted parts of the self, so that when they make their presence felt in the young person, there can be a possibility to make room for them.

Bibliography

Akhtar, S. (2009). *Comprehensive dictionary of psychoanalysis*. London: Routledge.

Alvarez, A. (1990). The close world of suicide. In *The savage god* (pp. 99–109). New York, NY: W. W. Norton & Company.

Bion, W. (1967). *Second thoughts: selected papers on psychoanalysis*. New York, NY: Jason Aronson Inc.

Bollas, C. (2018). *Meaning and melancholia: life in the age of bewilderment*. New York, NY: Routledge.

Buechler, S. (2000). Necessary and unnecessary losses. *Contemporary Psychoanalysis, 36*: 1, 77–90. DOI: 10.1080/00107530.2000.10747046

Campbell, D. (2008). The father transference in a pre suicide state. In S. Briggs and A. Lemma, (Eds.), *Relating to self-harm and suicide*. (pp. 25–35). New York, NY: Routledge.

Durkheim, E. (2002). *Suicide. A Study in Sociology*. (J. A. Spaulding and G. Simpsos, Trans.). London, England: Routledge & Kegan Paul. (Original work published 1951).

E Times (12 October, 2018). India is the 6th most depressed country: WHO report. Retrieved from https://timesofindia.indiatimes.com/life-style/health-fitness/de-stress/india-is-the-6th-most-depressed-country-who-report/articleshow/66179026.cms

Eigen, M. (1986). Mindlessness. In *The Psychotic Core*. (pp. 101–138). Northvale, NJ: Jason Aronson Inc.

Erikson, E. H. (1968). Prologue. In *Identity, youth and crisis*. (pp. 15–43). New York, NY: W.W. Norton & Company, Inc.

Erikson, E. H. (1968). Foundations in observation. In *Identity, youth and crisis*. (pp. 44–90). New York, NY: W.W. Norton & Company.

Frederickson, Jon. (2013). *Co-Creating Change: effective dynamic therapy techniques*. Kansas City, USA. Seven Leaves Press.

Freud, A. (1958). Adolescence. *The Psychoanalytic Study of the Child, 13*: 1, 255–278. DOI: 10.1080/00797308.1958.11823182

Freud, S. (1910d). The future prospects of psychoanalytic therapy. In *The standard edition of the complete psychological works of Sigmund Freud* (Vol. XI, pp. 139–152). London: Hogarth.

Freud, S. (1912b). The dynamics of transference. In *The standard edition of the complete psychological works of Sigmund Freud* (Vol. XII, pp. 97–108). London: Hogarth.

Freud, S. (1914g). Remembering, repeating, and working through In *The standard edition of the complete psychological works of Sigmund Freud* (Vol. XII, pp. 145–156). London: Hogarth.

Freud, S. (1964). *The standard edition of the complete psychological works of Sigmund Freud.* J. Strachey (Ed.). Oxford, England: Macmillan.

Freud, S. (1995). The economic problem of masochism. In M. Hanly (Ed.), *Essential papers on masochism.* (pp. 274–285). New York University Press. (Original paper published 1942).

Freud, S. (2003). Beyond the pleasure principle. In J. Reddick (Ed.), *Beyond the pleasure principle and other writings.* (pp. 43–102). London, England: Penguin Books. (Original work published 1920).

Freud, S. (2003). The uncanny. In D. McLintock, (Ed.), *The uncanny.* (pp. 121–161). London, England: Penguin Books. (Original work published 1919).

Freud, S. (2005). Drive and their fates. In G. Frankland (Ed.), *The unconscious.* (pp. 47–85). London, England: Penguin Books. (Original paper published in 1915).

Freud, S. (2005). Mourning and melancholia. In S. Whiteside (Ed.), *On murder, mourning and melancholia.* (pp. 201–218). London, England: Penguin Books. (Original work published 1917).

Garai, S. (29 January, 2020). Student suicides rising, 28 lives lost every day. *The Hindu.* Retrieved from https://www.thehindu.com/news/national/student-suicides-rising-28-lives-lost-every-day/article30685085.ece

Green, A. (1999). The death drive, negative narcissism and the disobjectalsing function. In A. Welter (Ed.), *The work of the negative.* (pp. 81–88). London, England: Free Association Books.

Green, A. (2005). Transference and counter transference. *In Key ideas for a contemporary psychoanalysis.* (pp. 43–58). New York, NY: Routledge.

Kernberg, O. F. (1999). Introduction. In A. Welter (Ed.), *The work of the negative.* (pp. xiii–xvii). London, England: Free Association Books.

Kernberg, O. F. (2009). The concept of the death drive: A clinical perspective. *International Journal of Psychoanalysis, 90,* 1009–1023. DOI: 10.1111/j.1745-8315.2009.00187.x

Lacan, J. (1978). The deconstruction of the drive in Sheridan. In *The four fundament concepts of psychoanalysis.* (pp. 161–173). New York, NY: W.W. Norton & Company.

Laplanche, J. (1976). Aggressiveness and sadomasochism. In (Mehlman, J., Trans.), *Life and death in psychoanalysis.* (pp. 85–102). Baltimore, MD: The Johns Hopkins University Press.

Layton, L. (2007). What psychoanalysis, culture and society mean to me. *The Academia-Industry Symposium MSM 2007: Medical Practice And The Pharmaceutical Industry. And Ever The Duo Shall Meet* (A.R. Singh and S.A. Singh Eds.), *MSM,* 5 Jan -Dec 2007, 146–157.

Maltsberger, J. T. (2004). The descent into suicide. In, *International Journal of Psychoanalysis 85*: 3, 653–668.

Mandar, H. (30 January, 2017). Mourning rohith vemula, who could not rescue himself from the 'fatal accident' of his birth. *The Wire.* Retrieved from https://thewire.in/books/mourning-rohith-vemula

Nandy, A. (1999). Sati: a nineteenth century tale of women, violence and protest. In T. G. Vaidyanathan and J. J. Kripal (Eds.), *Vishnu on Freud's desk: a reader in psychoanalysis and Hinduism*. New Delhi, India: Oxford University Press.

Paiva, N. D. (13 November, 2017). *Love and rage: the inner worlds of children*. New Delhi, India: Yoda Press.

Paiva, N. D. (13 November, 2020). Far away is the rainbow. *The Hindu Business Line*. Retrieved from https://www.thehindubusinessline.com/blink/cover/far-away-is-the-rainbow/article33090554.ece

Parker, I. (2015). Introduction. In *Psychology after psychoanalysis: psychosocial studies and beyond*. (pp. 1–8). New York, NY: Routledge.

Phillips, A. (1993). On risk and solitude. In *On kissing, tickling, and being bored*. (pp. 27–41). Cambridge, MA: Harvard University Press.

Rampal, N. (4 September, 2020). More than 90,000 young adults died by suicide in 2019 in India: NCRB report. *India Today*. Retrieved from https://www.indiatoday.in/diu/story/ncrb-report-data-india-young-adults-suicide-2019-india-1717887-2020-09-02

Rose, J. (2004). Introduction. In *Mass psychology and other writings*. (pp. vii–xxxix). London, England: Penguin Books.

Saha, D. (8 May, 2017). Every hour, one student commits suicide in India. *The Hindustan Times*. Retrieved from https://www.hindustantimes.com/health-and-fitness/every-hour-one-student-commits-suicide-in-india/story-7UFFhSs6h1HNgrNO60FZ2O.html

Schacter, J. (1999). The paradox of suicide: issues in identity and separateness. In S. Briggs and A. Lemma (Eds.), *Relating to self-harm and suicide*. (pp. 123–133). New York, NY: Routledge.

Sitlhou, M. (2017, November 21). India's universities are falling terribly short on addressing caste discrimination. *The Wire*. Retrieved from https://thewire.in/caste/india-universities-caste-discrimination

The Hindustan Times (20 January, 2016). *Suicides of Dalit students not new in Hyderabad University*. [press release] Retrieved from https://www.hindustantimes.com/india/suicides-of-dalit-students-not-new-in-hyderabad-university/story-cbPCCWPAF98q22uDihzb9L.html

The Indian Express (6 June, 2016). *Express RTI Application: NCRB figures show Highest Suicide Rates amongst Christians, Dalits and Tribals*. [press release]. Retrieved from https://indianexpress.com/article/india/india-news-india/express-rti-application-ncrb-figures-show-highest-suicide-rates-among-christians-dalits-tribals-2836677/

The Lancet (23 June, 2012). *Suicide Mortality in India: A Nationally Representative Survey* Retrieved from https://www.thelancet.com/journals/lancet/article/PIIS0140-6736(12)60606-0/fulltext

Verhaeghe, P. (2014). Identity. (J. Hedley-Prôle Trans.). In *What about me? The struggle for identity in a market based society*. (pp. 5–34). Australia: Griffen Press.

Webb, D. (13 May, 2013). *A collaborative approach to supporting people at risk for suicide.* [Webinar]. Mental Health Professional's Network. https://www.mhpn.org.au/WebinarRecording/16/A-Collaborative-Approach-to-Supporting-People-at-Risk-of-Suicide#.X-mBMi0RqCT

Whiteside, S. (2005). Translator's introduction. In *On murder, mourning and melancholia.* (pp. xxix- xxxiv). London, England: Penguin Books. (Original work published 1917).

Winnicott, D. (1949). Hate in counter transference. In *International Journal of Psycho-Analysis, 30*: 69–74.

Winnicott, D. (1960). Ego distortions in terms of true self and false self. In *The maturational processes and the facilitating environment: studies in the theory of emotional development.* (pp. 140–152). London, England: The Hogarth Press.

Winnicott, D. (1963). Communicating and not communicating leading to a study of certain opposites. In *The maturational processes and the facilitating environment: studies in the theory of emotional development.* (pp. 179–192) London, England: The Hogarth Press.

First WHO report on suicide prevention. (4 September, 2014). *World Health Organization.* Retrieved from http://www.who.int/mediacentre/news/releases/2014/suicide-prevention-report/en/

Wray, M., Colen, C., & Pescosolido, B. (2011). The sociology of suicide. In *Annual review of sociology, 37*: 505, 28.

About the Author

Ambika Singh is a trained psychoanalytic psychotherapist currently working at Family Tree: Child and Adolescent Mental Health Team in New Delhi, India. She has previously worked with mental health centres in universities, both private and public, to provide mental health services and support to young adults. After her BA in Psychology (Honours Programme) from Lady Shri Ram College for Women, Delhi University, she completed her MA in Psychology (Psychosocial Clinical Studies) and MPhil in Psychoanalytic Psychotherapy from Ambedkar University, Delhi. For almost a decade, Ambika has been working towards developing an understanding of suicidality, especially amidst Indian youth. Framed within the context of the alarming rise of suicide rates in India, her work as a psychotherapist and researcher reflects on the interpersonal nature of the feelings of suicidality.

Index

adolescence, 56–59
  Adam Phillip's view, 58
  Anna Freud's view, 56–57
  task for Adam Phillips, 130
adolescent, 59
affect deluge, 13
aggressiveness, 33
aggressivity, 35
alliance, 132
altruistic suicide, 6
Alvarez, A. (1999), 2
ambivalence, 33, 98
analytic association, 104–111
annihilation anxiety, 15
anomic suicide, 6
atmhatya/khud khushi, 8

Barred Subject, 31
'Beyond the Pleasure Principle', 19
  Second thoughts: selected papers on psychoanalysis, Bion, W., 1967, 15
blankness, 15
borderline splitting, 148
Branney 2008, 43

Cartesian subject, 31
cases
  C's
    analytic association, reflections, 84–88
    beginnings, 70–73
    confession and redemption, 77–81
    intimacy and identity, 75–76
    nature of suicidality, 81–84
    suicidal thoughts, 69
    trauma and controversy, 73–75
  P's, 111–126
    communication in Hindi, 112
    crazy behaviour, 113
    involvement within university, 116
    poetry, 114
    therapy, 111
  X's, 88–89
    dead/line, 101–104
    death and its images, 94–95
    diagnosis as deflection, 92–93
    initial encounter, 89–92
    moments of meeting, attempted, 99–101
    playing dead/terminating/ termination, 97–98
    reflections on the analytic association, 104–111
    working together and working alone, 95–97
caste struggles, 10, 144
Changes in psychoanalytic ideas, Cooper, A., 1987, 52
childhood experience, 138
class privilege, xix
clinical sensibility, 66
communication, 149
community, 40, 45, 65
compassion, 120, 156
complementary countertransference, 53
compliance, 14
compulsion to repeat, 18–20, 80, 84, 156
concordant countertransference, 53
conscious alliance, 157
co-participant, 133

core complex, 15
countertransference, 52
 direct, 53
 objective, 52
 Paula Heimann's view, 52–53
COVID-19, 150, 153
critical agency, 18, 22, 23, 109
cultural ambivalences, 142

death by suicide, 9, 40
death drive
 concept, 24–29
 defined by Freud, 138
 ego, 139
 Kernberg's views, 139–140
 post-Freudian understanding,
  29–37
 tendencies, 141
 The Work of the Negative,
  Andre Green, 34
deficit, 7, 8
de-mergence, 26, 27, 28, 139
de-mergence of drives, 26
derivatives of the drive, 29
destructive energy, 28, 139
destructiveness, 33
Diagnostic and Statistical Manual
 (DSM), 1
dialectic, 1, 41, 46, 62
direct countertransference
 complementary, 53
 concordant, 53
disobjectalizing, 35
Douglas (1967), 7
drive impulses, 25, 26, 63, 139
drives, 19, 20, 24, 25, 26
Drives and Their Fates, 24
Durkheim, E., 5

Economic Problem of Masochism, 28
ego, 139
ego alterations, 26, 134
ego development, 143
ego ideal, 16, 18, 26

ego identity, 143
egoistic suicide, 6
 Mindlessness, Eigen's, M., 1986
  blankness and mindlessness in
   psychosis, 15
embodied experience, 157
emotional distress, 153, 154
emotional world, 154, 155
 Prologue, Erikson, E. H., 1968, 65
ethics of care, 42, 57, 65
external events, 137

False Self, 13, 14, 156
fantasy of fusion, 15
fatalistic suicide, 7
Fenichels, O., 52
field of the Other, 32
found created, 35
fractured self, 135, 150
free-floating attention, 49
Freudian Field, 30

Gill, M., 52
Givocchini, P., 53
Green, A., 34

Heimann, P., 52
historical moment, 62
hypersensitive receptivity, 138

Id, 26–28, 58, 63–64
identification, 26
identifying, 136, 144
identity
 crisis, 60–62, 142–146
identity confusion, 60–61, 121
identity crisis, 60–62, 142–146
identity development, 56, 144
identity element, 60, 61, 65
identity formation, 142, 145, 146
identity locations, 10, 145, 147
ideological simplification, 126, 144
Indian National Crime Record
 Bureau (2014), xxv

inherent unknowability, 17
inner identity, 144
integration, 6, 7
internal critic, 132, 158
internal discomfort, 157
internal distress, 130, 131, 137, 154
internal experience, 77, 157
International Classification of
      Diseases (ICD), 1
interplay of the drive, 20
interpsychic, 63
interrupted ego development, 156
interruption, 117, 124
intrapsychic, 34, 56, 63

Jouissance, 32, 34
Jung, C., 52

Kernberg, O., 39, 40

Lacan, J., 30–31
Lancet Report (2012), xxv
Laplanche, J., 32
Layton, L., 142
liberal arts university, 146
libidinal investment, 22
life history, 39, 40, 41, 42, 43, 51
lost object, 21, 22

make room, 121, 128–129, 134, 156,
      158
Maltsberger, J., 13
marginalization, 9, 10, 11, 141
marginalized, 41, 61
masochism, 24, 28, 140
McWilliams, N., 53
melancholia
      concept defined by Freud, 131
      ego, 24
      suicide, 21–24
melancholic, 22
Menninger, K., 14
Mental Health Care Bill, 4, 12, 16, 40
metapsychology, 24, 29, 46

minority population, 4
mirrorings, 145
mixed feelings, 156
moment of crisis, 10, 57, 126
mourning, 21, 36, 40, 56, 121

Nandy, A., 4, 5
narcissism, 18, 24, 36
narcissistic, 15, 23
narcissistic identifications, 23
National Crime Records Bureau, 4
negative narcissism, 36
negative therapeutic reaction, 26, 140
new normal, 154
nirvana principle, 27
non-judgemental, 158
not knowing, 50

objective countertransference, 52
Oedipus complex, 26
old automatic thought processes, 132
oppositional positions, 137

pandemic, 150, 153, 154
Parker, I., 42
partial drive, 28, 30, 32
partial object, 32
passive position, 84, 107, 132
petit a, 31
Phillips, A., 58, 59, 130
pleasure principle, 19, 24, 25, 32, 139
praan tyaagna/iccha mrityu, 8
primal sadism, 28
Primary Masochism, 33
problem of representation, 17
projection of will, 159
psychic apparatus, 18, 19, 25, 139
psychic conflict, 35, 36
psychoanalysis, 12–16, 49–50
psychoanalytic tool box, 48–55
      listening, importance, 49–50
      transference and
            countertransference, 50–55
psychological mindedness, xix, xviii

psychosis, 22, 37, 133
psychosocial, 62–68
public clinic, xv, xvi

radical selection, 143
reality principle, 25
regulation, 6
relational dynamic, 104, 158
relational loss, 134
relational problem, 142
reliably present, 49
repetition, 29, 30, 34, 78, 140
repetition compulsion, 34, 140
return to a prior state, 15, 111
Rohith Vemula's suicide, 10, 12, 147
role responsiveness, 54
Rose, J., 63

sadism, 24, 28, 34, 140
Schachter, J., 15
Section 309 of the Indian Penal
    Code, 4
self-aggression, 33
self-care, 12, 157
self-destruction, 13, 142, 156
self-destructive, 140–141
self-work, 158
sexual drives, 25
social context, 141
social factors, 5, 7, 62, 64
social milieu, 61, 62, 64, 65, 126, 143
social ties, 6, 155
socio-political context, 62, 81, 142
socio-political forces, 49, 157
Strachey, J., 52
subject position, 9, 12, 16, 17, 42, 43,
    137, 146
subjecticide, 150
sublimation, 26, 28, 139
suicidal, 2
suicidal behaviour disorder, 2
suicidal ideation, 2, 41
suicidal intent, xiv
suicidal subject, 1, 13, 16

suicidal thoughts, 12, 17, 41, 69
suicidality
    brainstorming, 127–128
    concept of melancholia, 131
    nature of crisis, 129
    nature of transference, 129–138
    reflections on university clinic,
        146–148
    thematic continuities, 129–138
    understanding, 148–151
suicide, 1
    altruistic, 6
    anomic, 6
    article by Ashis Nandy, 4–5
    Beyond the Pleasure Principle, 19
    concept of death drive, 24–29
    data for India, 3–4
    definition by *Oxford English
        Dictionary*, 2–4
    diagnosis by DSM V, 2
    Douglas's theory, 7–8
    Durkheim's work, 4–8
    ego, 24
    egoistic, 6
    evolving question to research,
        39–43
    fallacies, 3
    fatalistic, 7
    Freud's views, 17–21
    ICD 9, defined, 2
    law/culture/society, 4–8
    melancholia, 21–24
    National Crime Records
        Bureau, 4
    pleasure principle, defined by
        Freud, 19
    psychiatric framework, 1
    psychoanalytic tool box, 48–55
    questions and setting, 45–48
    research in university, 9–12
    research towards engage with
        evolving question, 39–43
    psychosocial understanding,
        62–68

sample nature, 55–62
setting up setting, 43–45
uncanny, defined by Freud, 18
Super Ego, 23, 26, 27
supervision, 46, 158

The Work of the Negative, 34
transference
    false connection by Freud, 50
    interpretation, 52
    neurosis, 51
    Studies on Hysteria, Freud, 50
transference interpretation, 52
transferrential dynamic, 129
Trieb, 29
true self, 13–14

uncanny, 18–20, 24
unconscious, 24, 25
unconscious axiom, 149
unintended repetition, 18

university, 9–12
    clinic within, 12–16
    Descent into Suicide,
        John Maltsberger, 13
    psychoanalysis and suicide,
        12–16
    Psychoanalytic Aspects of Suicide,
        Karl Menninger, 14
    suicide site, 9–12
university clinic, 146–148
unpleasure, 29, 32, 51, 83, 84, 109

Verhaeghe, P., 145

willing, 25, 61, 83, 84, 123
Winnicott, D., 52, 58, 59, 136,
    156
witness, ix, viii, xii, xiv, xvi

youth, 9, 65, 83, 148, 154
youth in India, 153